Ottawa Stories

Ottawa Stories

TRIALS & TRIUMPHS IN BYTOWN HISTORY

CLIFF SCOTT

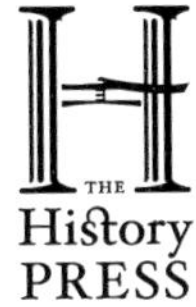

Published by The History Press
Charleston, SC 29403
www.historypress.net

First published 2014

Printed in Canada

ISBN 978.1.62619.341.3

Library of Congress CIP data applied for.

Notice: The information in this book is true and complete to the best of our knowledge. It is offered without guarantee on the part of the author or The History Press. The author and The History Press disclaim all liability in connection with the use of this book.

Contents

Introduction

I first saw Ottawa from a train window in the spring of 1954 when I reported for duty in the Royal Canadian Air Force (RCAF). I saw the Parliament buildings from the Hull side of the river (as it was then), surrounded by fresh greenery, and I fell in love. Except for going west for a while for postings and schooling, this city has been my home ever since.

Fishing, swimming, sleigh rides and hiking have been a part of my life, as well as marrying "a girl from the valley" and raising a family. I have worked here, earned my living, coached baseball and grew even fonder of my city over time. Sharing local stories at family "pig roasts," learning local history, running a small museum and getting immersed in local heritage gave me an even better feel for the place and an incentive to tell others about Ottawa.

This is, therefore, an attempt to pull together a local background and share stories. It is not a formal or official history but rather an inspiration to those who want to know more. If a story intrigues you, then I hope you will go to one of the sources identified, or others like them, and learn more about people and things that have made Ottawa a fascinating, historical and simply wonderful place to live.

A special thanks to my son and daughter, who helped gather pictures, research and type, as well as to my wife, who put up with an old curmudgeon while the book was being written.

Part I
The Birth of Bytown

Early Origins of Ottawa

As far as the First Nations are concerned, archaeologists tell us that there are sites dating back to circa 8000 BCE. The Ottawa and St. Lawrence Rivers were a dividing line for native people in the sense that the Iroquois nations lived south of the St. Lawrence, the Hurons west of the Ottawa and the Algonquins north and east of the Ottawa. These were not hard-and-fast dividing lines, and there was surely some spillover between the areas that caused conflict from time to time. During the French regime, the Ottawa was the highway to the fur-producing areas to the northwest. This continued after the English took over in 1763, and the Ottawa also became the highway for the timber trade, which was really to blossom in the mid-eighteenth century. A navigational instrument belonging to Samuel de Champlain was discovered not far from Ottawa dating back to the early seventeenth century. The songs and "chanteys" of the voyageurs were probably some of the only sounds heard along the river for close to two hundred years.

In the early seventeenth century, the rivers also served as the route that Jesuit missionaries took to live among the Hurons at "Ste. Marie Among the Hurons," until the mission was destroyed by the Iroquois in 1634. For various reasons too complex to mention here, the Iroquois always tended to side with the British. This was the case even after the United States declared independence in 1776. The situation changed near Ottawa after 1783, when the United States became fully independent of Britain and a group of people known as United Empire Loyalists began to settle along the St. Lawrence and up country from there. These were people who had supported Britain during the war from 1776 to 1783 and, with the exception of in South Carolina, were no longer welcome in the United States. Their lands and properties were expropriated for U.S. supporters, and they had to seek new homes. Land was made available to them in Eastern Ontario by the British government.

These land grants grew after the War of 1812 as the British government wanted the land taken up by those loyal to Britain and not likely to join the republic to the south. These settlements were supported by Sir Guy Carleton, governor of Canada until 1796, who was aided by Sir Evan Nepean of the British colonial office. Their names are still evident in the area today. In 1791, there were only 20,000 settlers in all of Upper Canada compared to 130,000 in Quebec. This was another reason English people were wanted in the area and the next settlement waves supported this policy before 1826. A number of people came up from Vermont. Some of the native names appearing on those treaties are amusing choices: Shabisi ("a rough bird"), Kakadas ("big mud fish") and Nitwasinini ("a windy man"). One can only guess why someone was called a windy man.

Settlers came in from many lands and for varied reasons—Highland Scots from the clearances; Irish for canal work and later because of the potato famine; veterans of the Napoleonic wars; Irish protestants, who settled near Almonte; and Scottish and English to work on the Rideau Canal. Aside from land records, there are historical sources for the names of the settlers in most of the areas around Ottawa. *Belden's Historical Atlas of 1879* even shows where people settled in detail. Gourlay's 1892 *History of the Ottawa Valley* gives much detailed information but is incredibly difficult to use as it has no chapters or table of contents and is just a continuous narrative from beginning to end. *Carleton Saga* (a more recent book, produced in 1968) along with G. Lockwood's histories of certain townships are further sources of information. Wherever they came from, they were the impetus for the stories that follow—from semi-legendary figures like Big Joe Mufferaw and Mother McGinty to historical figures such as John By and more modern personalities like the controversial mayor of Ottawa Charlotte Whitton. It's a pleasure to tell their stories!

The Early Settlers and Their Stories

Some of the names that have come down to us are given in a following section, so perhaps readers can determine if they are descended from some of these first people. Carleton County, where Ottawa rests, was established by an act of King George III, and great detail is available in H. Belden's historical atlas and Gourlay's history. Bytown, which became Ottawa in 1854, was the principal town in the county. Soldiers appear first—veterans of the Napoleonic wars and the War of 1812. They were encouraged to settle in Upper Canada, especially near the border with the United States in case there was an encore of the War of 1812.

The first recorded political representative of the British government was Colonel Burke of His Majesty's 99th Regiment in Brockville. Other military names that appear include Colonels Lyons and Lewis near Richmond, as well as Malloch, Stewart, Pinhey and James Johnston. Nonmilitary names include Ormsby, Street, Edwards, Aumond, Stephenson, McKinnon, McTaggart, Fenton, Freeman, Petry, Bradley, Durie, Hinton, Pinhey and McElroy. Other military names appear in 1854, associated with the 1st Rifles: Patterson, Fraser, Abbott, Grant, May, Mowat, Esmonde, McCuaig and Lang. In the town of Bytown in 1832, right after the canal was completed, we find Colonel John By, who arrived in September 1826, accompanied by J. Clowe, who designed the route of the canal. There was also Caleb T. Bellows, who had a dock and a general store prior to 1820, and Nicholas Sparks, who was from across the river in Wrightville.

Isaac Firth and his wife had a tavern. Firth had come to Canada from Yorkshire and married the intrepid Miss Dalmahoy, who had come to Canada in 1818 by herself to work as a milliner. She arrived at the foot of the Chaudière Falls after a long trip from Edinburgh, with all the usual stops along the way. Historian Robert Leggett says nothing about how Isaac met his bride and nothing about what happened to them before the canal was begun. He noted that "she had fame in making black otter caps for the workers on the canal and that skill was only rivalled by the conviviality of the entertainment at the bar, known far and wide as 'Mother Firth's.'" I wonder how much competition existed between Mother Firth's and Mother McGinty's for the drinking crowd. Nicholas Sparks was a young Irishman when he married the widowed daughter-in-law of Philemon Wright (1760–1839), who founded the Quebec city of Hull (now Gatineau) and had enough money to buy land that he then sold to build the canal, no doubt at a handsome profit.

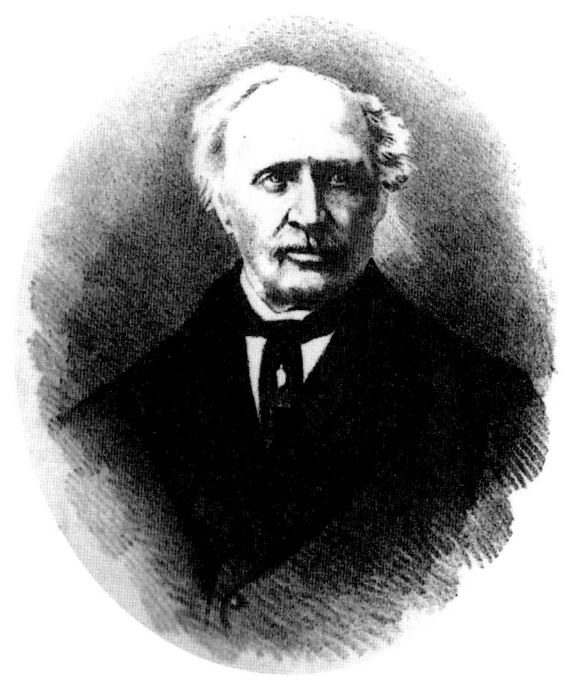

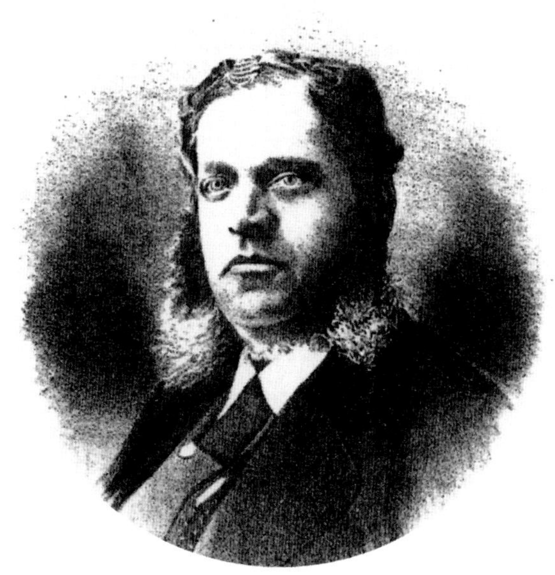

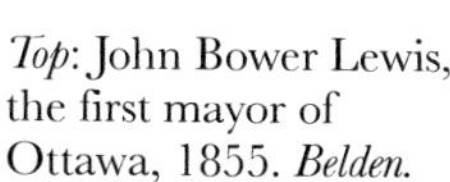

Top: John Bower Lewis, the first mayor of Ottawa, 1855. *Belden.*

Right: A portrait of an early Ottawa settler. *Belden.*

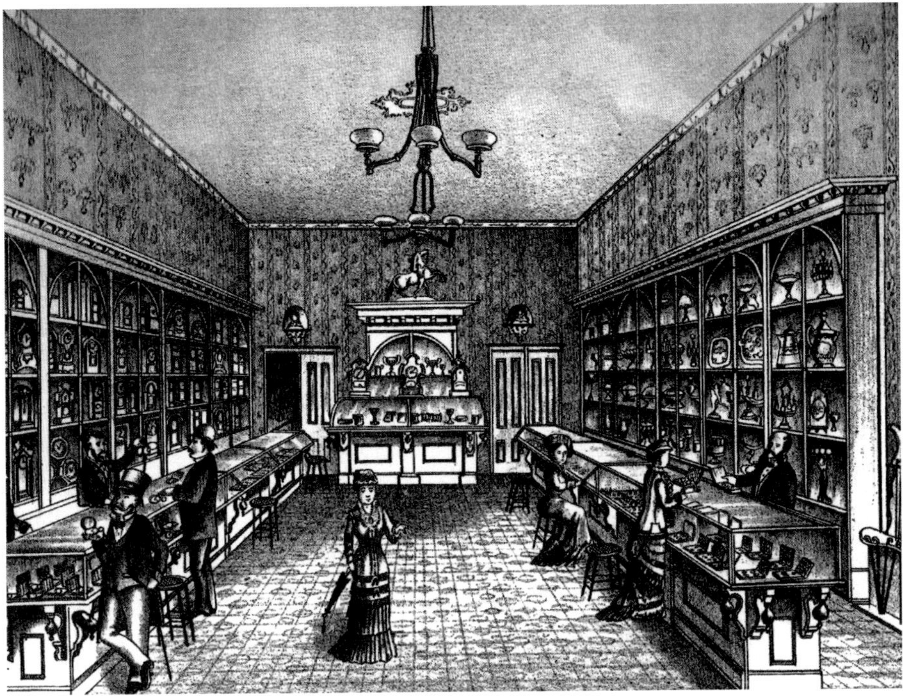

The interior of a jewelry store, image taken in 1879. *Belden.*

The story of Lamira Dow Billings, the wife of Bradish Billings, is even more interesting. She was the daughter of a United Empire Loyalist (UEL) who personally survived a trip over the Hog's Back falls together with her infant daughter, Sabra. She went on to have more children, making the Billings name well known throughout the area.

The present-day area from Laurier to the Sapper's bridge was known as Corktown. Most of the town was swamp (i.e., Dow's Lake), and Parliament Hill was a densely wooded hemlock ridge. By 1828, though, Belden estimated that there were fifteen general stores, three jewelry stores, eight shoemakers and three blacksmiths. There were at least four pubs, including the Russell House and the Windsor Arms, which was still standing in 1969–70.

In the New Edinburgh neighbourhood, Thomas McKay, builder of Rideau Hall, took up residence and had nine children; one daughter married T.C. Keefer, a celebrated engineer. Before 1842, the following names appear: Allen, Askwith, Blackburn, Burritt, Brennan, Ballantyne, Henry, Scott and Sherwood. In the suburb of Richmond, named after the Duke of Richmond, who tragically died of hydrophobia while visiting the

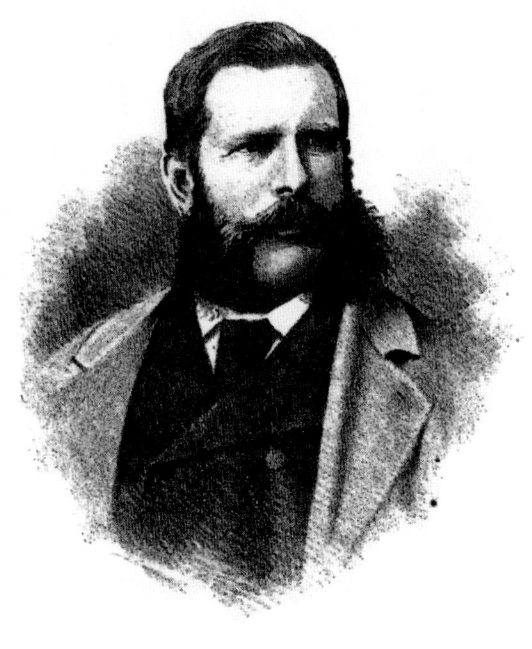

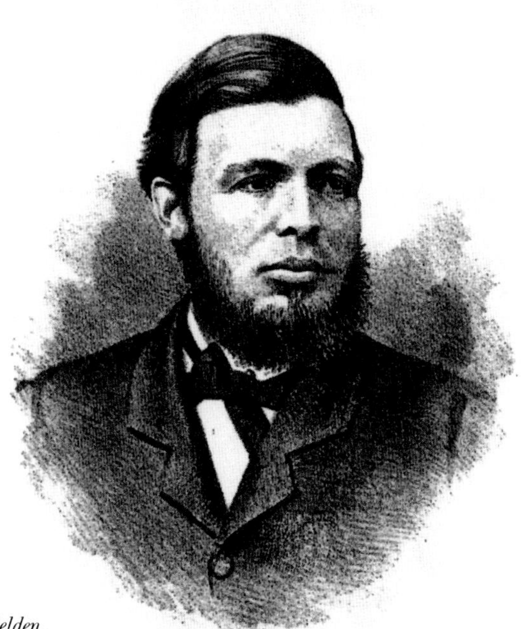

Portraits of early Ottawa settlers. *Belden*.

area, officers and men of the 99th and 100th Regiments of the line, veterans of the Napoleonic Wars, were settled in 1818. Some names included Taylor, Dennison, Burke, Lyon and a host of others.

In the township of Nepean, which was first surveyed in 1798, the following names appear: Sherwood, McLaughlin and Honeywell. Mary Honeywell ran the first school in the area, and Peter Honeywell, who manages Ottawa's Arts Court, is a direct descendant. The Dow and Moore families appear also. Lamira Dow married Bradish Billings and was one of the first settlers of Gloucester Township. Their original house still stands as part of the Billings estate museum. The Henrys were also early settlers. One of the Henrys was a raftsman on the Ottawa River and married Jane Birch, who also came from an early Nepean family.

United Empire Loyalists

Many of the early settlers in the Ottawa region and to the south originated among United Empire Loyalists, and their descendants are still active today. The history of the UEL is a fascinating one and not really too well known to today's citizens. Hence, here are a very few words on the origins of the name and what they went through more than 230 years ago, as well as the impact they had on Canada.

During what they call the American Revolutionary War and what our American friends call the American War of Independence, not all residents of what is now the United States supported the idea of independence from Britain. There were a variety of reasons for this rejection, and elaborating on them would require a book in itself. Suffice it to say, they were on the losing end when peace was restored between Britain and the United States in 1783. However, much of the UEL's distaste for the republican ideals of the United States and also the treatment they received from the country were never forgotten. As to the former, one Loyalist has been quoted as saying that it would be better to be dictated to by one tyrant one thousand miles away rather than by one thousand tyrants one mile away.

The UEL were not really welcome in the United States, and some Americans made life very uncomfortable for them in addition to the expropriation of their land and businesses to partially compensate themselves for losses suffered in the war, which had gone on since 1776. Some of the biggest "losers" were the tribes of the Iroquois Confederation, who backed the British. Their lands became open for settlement, and many headed north to Canada, where they settled near Brantford, Ontario, and Montreal, Quebec.

The British governors of Canada made land available to them, a minimum of two hundred acres to be more precise, plus an equal amount to their sons when they reached the age of majority. They settled on the north shore of the St. Lawrence River and gradually filled up the hinterland to the north. Many of the settlers in the townships around what became Ottawa were UELs or were descended from them. The old tradition of dislike for the United States died hard.

Suspicions about the aims of the United States were heightened by the War of 1812, the concept of Manifest Destiny and the Fenian Raids that predated Confederation. While the latter were not policies of the United States government, the fact that they were carried out by U.S. citizens could not be denied. (By way of explanation and discussed in some depth later in the book, Fenians were Irishmen, many of them veterans of the U.S. Civil War, who invaded Canada in the hope of capturing the then British colony and trading it for home rule in Ireland.) Since those long-ago days, there has been a consistent minority who wanted nothing to do with the United States, and organizations still exist that worry about U.S. intentions and lobby against U.S. culture, political influence and economic domination.

THE RIDEAU CANAL

The Rideau Canal—the catalyst that created Bytown (which became Ottawa), a World Heritage Site and a great waterway for boating—turned 175 years old in 2007. It was originally planned as a major military highway running from Ottawa to Kingston, bypassing rapids and the possibility of American invasion. It was foreseen that boats would come from Montreal to Bytown and then to Kingston. Montreal and Kingston were well settled by 1820, but the area around what would become Ottawa was still wilderness, except for Philemon Wright's settlement across the Ottawa River in Quebec. Wright had settled there in 1800 and piloted the first square timber raft downriver in 1806.

Opened in 1832, the Rideau Canal is the oldest continuously operating canal system in North America. The canal system is two hundred kilometres in length and uses sections of major rivers, including the Rideau and the Cataraqui, as well as some lakes. Only nineteen kilometres or thereabouts are man-made. It is still used today for pleasure boating, with most of the original structure intact. The locks on the system open for navigation in mid-May and close in mid-October. There are forty-seven locks to navigate in the full course of the canal.

In 1925, the Rideau Canal was designated a National Historic Site of Canada. Plaques were installed in 1926 and again in 1962. It was later designated a Canadian Heritage River. Finally, it was acknowledged as a UNESCO World Heritage Site in 2007 in recognition of it as a work of "creative human genius." At the same time, it gained credit as the best-preserved example of a slack water canal in North America. It is the only canal dating from the great North American canal building era of the nineteenth century that remains operational along its original route and with most of its original structures intact. It incorporates forty-seven locks, sixteen lakes, two rivers and a 360-foot, 60-foot-high dam at Jones Falls, which was completed in 1832 so the canal could be opened. Many communities border the waterway, including Ottawa, Manotick, Burrits Rapids, Merrickville, Smith Falls, Rideau Ferry, Portland, Westport, Newboro, Seeley's Bay and Kingston. Kemptville and Perth are connected by navigable waterways. Besides pleasure craft, boat tours are offered in Ottawa, Kingston, Merrickville and Chaffey's Locks. It connects Montreal with the great lakes and their watershed.

Most of the locks are still hand operated. There are forty-five locks at twenty-three stations along the canal, plus two locks at the entrance to the Tay Canal, which leads to the town of Perth. Furthermore, there are four blockhouses and some of the original lockmasters' houses found along the route. Their houses were made defensible in case of a military attack. In normal operations, the canal can handle boats up to 27.4 metres (90 feet) in length, 7.9 metres (26 feet) in width and 6.7 metres (22 feet) in height, with a draft of up to 1.5 metres (4 feet). The canal was constructed between 1826 and 1832, and the project was managed by Lieutenant Colonel John By of the British Royal Engineers. Little did he know that it would be used as one of the world's most unique skateways.

In winter, a section of the Rideau Canal passing through Ottawa is converted into the world's largest skating rink and park. The cleared rink is 7.8 kilometres square (4.8 miles) and has a surface area equivalent to ninety

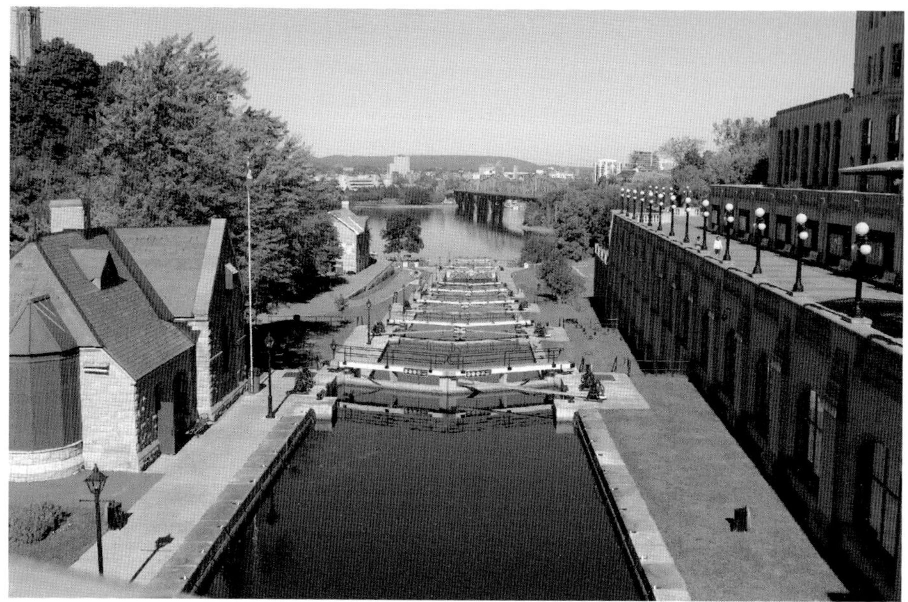

Modern entrance to the Rideau Canal in downtown Ottawa. *Author's collection.*

Olympic skating rinks. It runs from Carleton University to the locks between the Parliament buildings and the Chateau Laurier, including the whole of Dow's Lake. It serves as a popular tourist attraction and recreational area and specializes in a popular local snack: the beavertail, a fried flat dough pastry the size of a five- by seven-inch picture frame that comes in many flavours, such as rolled in white sugar and cinnamon or topped with hot apple pie filling. The skateway is open twenty-four hours a day, and the season typically lasts from January until March. It has opened as early as January 1 and stayed open as late as March 12.

As late as the 1970s, the city government considered paving over the canal to create an expressway, but it was frustrated by the fact that the canal was owned by the federal government. It was the head of the National Capital Commission, a federal agency, who suggested the use of the canal as a skateway. On January 18, 1971, Douglas Fullerton proudly realized his dream and opened the canal. Fifty thousand people showed up for the event, and despite his achievement, Colonel By was summoned back to London to explain the cost overrun—the final cost was £822,000, approximately £135,000 higher than the original estimate. Although he was absolved of all blame, he was never honoured by the British government, and it has remained for the citizens of the city he founded to name streets after him, erect statues in his memory, name a day after him and have him guide visitors along his canal (actors, of course). The historical society pays the cost of perpetual care for his grave site in Sussex in the United Kingdom.

The monetary cost was overwhelming, but what about other costs, aside from money and fame? How many died as a result of the canal's construction? How many became ill with the diseases of the time and might have suffered lifelong effects? These questions have only partial answers. As many as one thousand workers died from malaria alone. Accidents were fairly rare, but in 1827, seven accidental deaths were recorded. All who died were buried in local cemeteries or in burial grounds set up near the worksites. Funerals were held for the workers, and graves were marked with wooden crosses. Many of the markers have disappeared over time, leading to a misconception that many were buried in unmarked graves. Thanks to the efforts of the Ottawa and Kingston Labour Councils, as well as the Ontario Heritage Foundation, memorials have been erected at Ottawa, Kingston and Chaffey's Locks.

The canal was a monumental undertaking for its time and was completed quickly and almost within cost—a credit to those who built it. It has served the area well for many years as a military highway, a transportation route for settlers, a quiet cruising ground in the nineteenth century and a haven for pleasure boats and skaters in more modern times. It is truly a part of our heritage to be honoured by all. For those who appreciate technical details, here is some basic information:

- lock dimensions: 134 by 33 feet
- draft: a minimum of 5 feet
- in Ottawa: 131 feet above sea level
- in Kingston: 246 feet above sea level
- the lift from Ottawa to the Upper Rideau Lake is 277 feet through thirty-three locks; the lift from Upper Rideau Locks to Kingston is 162 feet through fourteen locks

Part II
Characters

Lieutenant Colonel John By, Royal Engineers

Known as the founder of Bytown (or Ottawa, as it eventually became known), John By was an accomplished construction engineer with several major projects to his credit before supervising the construction of the Rideau Canal between 1826 and 1832. Elsewhere, comment is made on the influence that the canal had on the growth of Bytown. Robert Leggett's work on the construction of the canal should be consulted for those who wish for more detail. The pamphlet on Colonel By produced by the Historical Society of Ottawa is equally informative. A statue that is said to be a good likeness stands in Major's Hill Park, overlooking the first eight locks in the canal. By's storehouse (or commissariat), the oldest stone building in the city, sits across from his statue.

By was born in 1799 in London, England, the son of a family of British public servants largely employed by the customs service. John, a second son, moved from the customs service to the military. He attended the Royal Military Academy at Walswick and was commissioned in 1799 in the Royal Artillery; in later years, he would be transferred to the Royal Engineers. In March 1805, he attained the rank of captain. He had been posted to

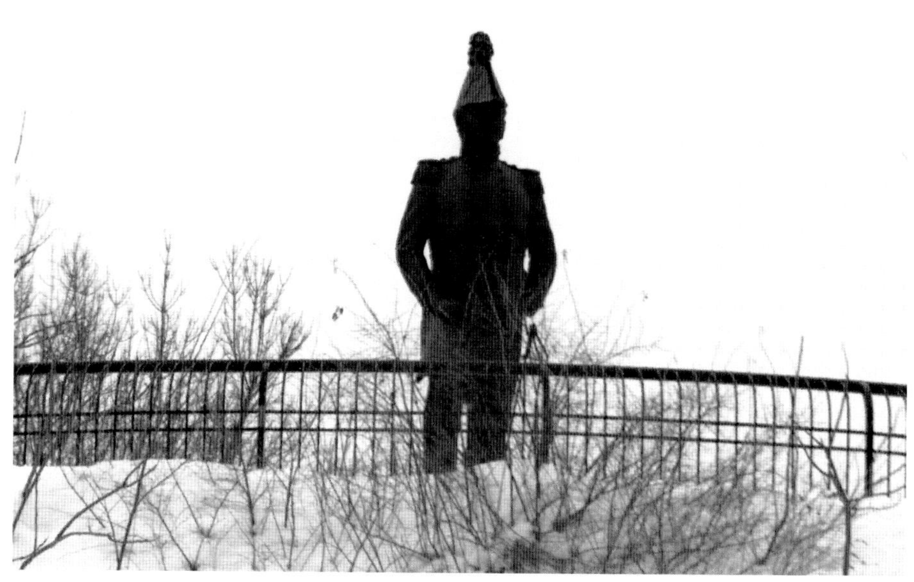

Statue of Colonel Jon By, the founder of Bytown. *Author's collection.*

Canada in 1802 and stayed until he was recalled to Europe in 1811 for service in Spain and Portugal, now as a senior captain. In his first posting to Canada, he served in Quebec City and was occupied with enhancing the fortifications at Quebec and in the construction of the first small canal at the Cedan on the St. Lawrence River. It is probable that he travelled much in Canada during his first posting.

He served with distinction in the Peninsular War, taking part at the Siege of Badajoz, where he might have come to the attention of the Duke of Wellington. Returning to England, he was assigned to important posts in the manufacture of gunpowder and small arms at Favershan, Purefleet and Waltham Abbey from 1812 until 1821. He was promoted to major and then to lieutenant colonel after he was placed on the unemployed list owing to reductions in the army at the end of the Napoleonic Wars. His accomplishments and experience were such that he was appointed to supervise the construction of the Rideau Canal in 1826, perhaps with a recommendation from the Duke of Wellington himself.

Colonel By was married twice. His first wife died shortly after the marriage. There were no children from this union. He then married Elizabeth March in 1818 while stationed at Waltham Abbey. They had two daughters, both of whom came to Canada with their parents. One daughter later married, but her children died without issue, so there are no direct descendants of Colonel By.

Leggett described By as about five feet, ten inches in height and very stout ("almost to the point of corpulence"). He had dark hair and a florid complexion. He was good-natured in character, with a good sense of humour. His home, above the eight entrance locks to the canal, later caught fire in 1849, so there is no drawing or precise description of its exterior and interior except for a few brief descriptions and some archaeological work. However, it is mentioned in a letter reprinted in Leggett's seminal work by Frances Simpson, a visitor: "The house which stands in a good garden, overlooks one of the most beautiful spots I have seen in the whole country; it commands an extensive view of the river on the opposite side of which is the little village of Hull."

Not only did the writer pay compliments to Mrs. By and her house, but also she commented favourably on the surrounding landscape, much of which had been developed by Colonel By. By also had to be the chief legal officer until a magistrate was appointed, and Leggett related an interesting story of how By had to invade the premises of a bakery that was involved in illegal alcohol sales. By himself was arrested by the deputy sheriff as an "instigator of a riot." We are left hanging as to the outcome of the charge.

The tale of Colonel By's construction of the canal and its technology and impact on the area is marred by the financial difficulties that darkened the final stages of his career. The canal wound up costing even more than revised estimates, and By was held accountable for the cost overruns (something that rarely happens even today). While it is rumored that he expected to be knighted for his great accomplishment, as he was admired by many, the financial cloud hanging over the final cost was apparently enough to prevent this recognition.

Colonel By, after finishing his work, retired to his estate in Front Sussex, where he died within a few years, unrecognized. The Historical Society of Ottawa commissioned a statue to be placed overlooking his commissariat and pays for the perpetual maintenance of his grave. The City of Ottawa named the first Monday in August "Colonel By Day" in his honour.

Big Joe Mufferaw

A lot of people think that Joe was a legend. There are even some who say that he was the model for Paul Bunyan, the legendary North Woods logger. In his book *The Lumberjacks*, Donald MacKay has the following to say about it, quoting Charlie MacCormick of Port Menier, Anticosti: "My God, my grandfather worked with him! He and my grandfather, Michael MacCormick, rafted wood on the Ottawa River. Together! Sure!" So, the song sung by Stompin' Tom Connors tells a real story, even allowing for a little poetic license: "...He was fair-haired and blue-eyed and very popular with the ladies."

Joseph Montferrand (the English pronunciation of the French name led to the nickname "Mufferaw") was born in 1802 and grew up with the square timber trade. He died in October 1864 and is buried in Notre Dame des Neiges Cemetery in Montreal. He was a big man for his time, standing six feet, two inches, and was famous for his boxing prowess before he left Montreal to take part in the timber trade in Ottawa Valley and parts of Quebec. His origins were in the northeast of France. One of his favourite tricks was to do a backflip, during which he put the imprint of his logging boots on an eight-foot ceiling. The story is that he got his athletic ability and balance from his grandfather, who had been a fencing master. Joe is famous locally for two memorable fights on the bridge that spanned the Ottawa between Bytown and Hull. In one case, he is said to have held off a crowd of 150 "shiners" (Irish labourers) who had worked on the building of the Rideau Canal and were competing with the French Canadian "bucherons" for work in the timber industry. There are actually three famous stories of his "doings" in Ottawa, about the same time Colonel John By was getting the Rideau Canal built.

One night, Joe and his confreres were out drinking, probably in what is now Lower Town or in the Byward Market. There were certainly enough pubs to go around. They went to the pub of an old acquaintance only to find that the ownership had changed hands. Joe explained the situation to a new, pretty barmaid, noting that they had no money. She said that they could stay and be served because they looked like men of honour. Montferrand thanked her, and from the centre of the tavern, he did his famous backflip and kicked his boot marks into the ceiling to show that he had been there. It is said that visitors came from miles away to admire the work of Joe Montferrand, and the pub prospered. Maybe the mark is still there if you visit the right pub!

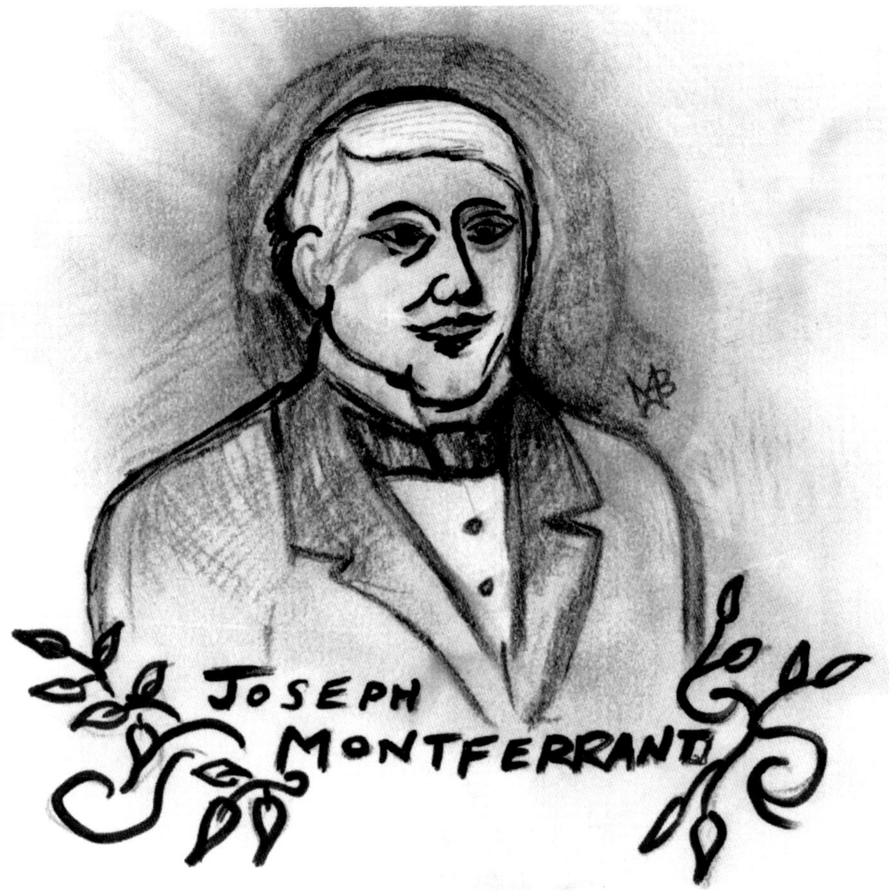

"Big Joe" Montferrand/Mufferaw drawing made from a wood cutout. *Mackay*.

Another story also involves a pretty girl. Joe was taken with this girl in Bytown and decided to court her. She was also interested in a large highlander named MacDonald, who had six large brothers. The seven MacDonalds decided to jump Big Joe to teach him a lesson. They cornered him on the Bytown side of the bridge to Hull. Joe grabbed a pole from the bridge and, swinging it like a club, damaged the seven brothers badly and drove them all off.

The competition between the "shiners" and the French Canadian "bucherons" was fierce. Joe was the leader of the French loggers, and the shiners decided that if they eliminated him, there would be work for them. According to Peter Mackay, it was in 1829 that the gang of

150 ambushed Joe on the same bridge, armed with clubs. Saying a little prayer, for the odds were pretty bleak, Joe walked forwards and picked up the largest Irishman by his feet. Swinging the gentleman like a club, Joe did terrible damage to the ranks of his enemies. The carnage was terrific, and wishing to avoid the same treatment, the balance of the shiners ran up the road.

There are only a few stories about the legendary logger. He was a character in early Bytown, but the fact that he actually existed is not disputed. There are stories of his life all over Eastern Ontario, just as with Johnny Appleseed, Daniel Boone and Davy Crockett, who were real people as well. Our friends to the south seem to do a much better job of remembering their heroes. Joseph Montferrand married at the age of sixty and had one son. He died quietly at home in Montreal (212 Rue Sanguine) on October 4, 1864.

MOTHER MCGINTY

This colourful character might have been real, as she was remembered fondly in the 1879 *Illustrated History of Carleton County* by H. Belden. There is, in fact, a descriptive poem written by Councilman Lett before 1879.

Mother McGinty ran a pub in Corktown, where the University of Ottawa is now located. There is a footbridge across the canal connecting the university with Somerset Street West named the Corktown Bridge in honour of the Irish labourers who worked on the canal. It is "upriver" from the Celtic Cross erected in memory of the workers who died in the construction of the canal.

Mother McGinty's system of accounting and her methods of dunning deadbeats could still be used today if we focused on personal responsibility a bit more than a system of political correctness (which might find her methods unacceptable). Today, Ottawa is still described by some as a place where the sidewalks are rolled up by 9:00 p.m. Our town was not always this way. In its earliest days, the days of free whisky in politics, there were no social agencies or institutions of social betterment. Belden's history and a poem composed by W.P. Lett, the city clerk, accurately describe conditions in the famous pub in 1828, and the latter is reproduced word for word on the following pages. The words are certainly descriptive:

Mother McGinty sat in state,
And measured out the mountain dew
To those who strong attraction drew
Within the circle of her power
To while away a leisure hour.
She was the hostess and the host;
She kept the reckoning, ruled the roast
And swung an arm of potent might
That few would dare to brave in fight;
Yet was she a good natured soul
As ever filled the flowing bowl
In sooth, she dealt in goodly cheer
Half pints of whiskey, quarts of beer
Strong doses of sweet peppermint,

Fine old Jamaica, without stint
And shrub, a cordial then well known
Her thirsty customers then poured down
Nor dreamed of headaches or of ills
For nought killed them save doctor's pills
For cash or credit bartered she
The prime ingredients of a spree
And he stood always above par
Who ne'er a stone threw at the bar
And when a man had spent his all
She chalked the balance on the wall
Figures or letters she knew naught
But what a customer had got
By hieroglyphics well she knew
For there, exposed to public view

Each debtor's tally, great or small.
Appeared, along the bar room wall
A short stroke for a half pint stood
A longer for a quart was good;
While something like an eagle's talon
Upon her blackboard was a gallon.

And was to him. Soon not late
His tally did not liquidate,
For when her goodly company
Were all assembled for a spree

She read off each delinquent's score
And at his meaness loudly swore
And threatened when he next appeared
Unless the entry all was cleared
To lay on future drinks a stricture
And lay our a fulsome picture

In pewter for the unpaid tally.
As five (I think) in C. O'Malley!

Ottawa had a reputation for hard living. It was a hard-drinking town for many years even after the canal was finished. Logging and lumbering took over from canal construction and kept the spirits flowing, and social disturbances will testify to that. Even in modern days, a prominent local political family named McGuinty might have some ancestral connection to Mother McGinty's days.

Part III
The Timber Town

Riotous Bytown

Bytown had a rough reputation before it officially became the city of Ottawa. There was always factional conflict ever since Joe Mufferaw took on the MacDonald boys over the affections of a special lady. In fact, the Ballygiblin Riots took place even before that. In 1823, under the sponsorship of a gentleman named Peter Robinson, Irish immigrants from northern Cork settled only a few miles up the valley, where the town of Almonte stands today. They were called "Ballygiblins" or "Corkers."

Military settlers had populated the area around Perth, which is not far away, and they were primarily of English and Scottish extraction. All settlers were given land grants, as well as farm tools, seed, grain and livestock, to start their farms, but the quantity and quality varied. There is a plaque on the site of the riot in the town of Carleton Place, known at the time of the riot as Morphy's Falls. The Perth settlers (mostly Protestant) and the Almonte settlers (mostly Catholic) were opposed on religious grounds and also concerning the goods given to the first settlers. The Protestants thought that the Irish had gotten more and were determined to do something about it. They marched towards Almonte and were met by the Irish at Morphy's Falls. Insults, rocks and anything else near at hand filled the air, and clubs were wielded over a period of time. The militia were called out to quell the riot, and peace eventually prevailed. This happened even before the canal was built.

Around Ottawa, you will often hear references to the "Shiner's War," which took place in Bytown between 1835 and 1845. It was essentially a war over jobs, as the Irish labourers hired to work on the canal looked for work after 1832. They cast their eyes on the timber trade, where most jobs were held by loggers and river men from Quebec, whose leader was Big Joe Mufferaw. The war started when Peter Aylen, a major Irish timber baron, organized a group of Irishmen to attack other timber operations. The group was known as the Shiners, probably derived from the French word *cheneur*, meaning a cutter of oak trees. The Shiners attacked French Canadian timber rafts and fought against the French on the streets of Bytown and in the Byward Market. The Shiners also attacked political institutions because Aylen aspired to political office, and he led his "troops" to secure position in the Agricultural Society and meetings in Nepean Township. He was repulsed from the latter.

The violence was so troublesome that the citizens established an association for the purpose of maintaining the peace that contained armed patrols to try and control the violence, but it still continued. In the spring of 1837, the government deployed troops to arrest the agitation, and violence was brought under control except for sporadic outbreaks by those claiming to be Shiners as late as 1845. This more or less finished the formal violence between the Irish and the French, but it did not change the view of Bytown as a violent place. Riots were still occurring, and when the loggers came to town, there was much rambunctious behavior.

The next occurrence of a major riot was the Stony Monday Riot of September 17, 1849. In April 1849, the governor, Lord Elgin, had signed the Rebellion Losses Bill to compensate Lower Canadians for losses suffered in the Rebellions of 1837–38. This did not sit well with the right-wing pro-British Tories, who saw French Canadians other than those convicted of treason who had participated in the Rebellion receiving benefits from the Crown. Riots followed in Montreal and then in the capital, and the Parliament buildings were burned. Lord Elgin let it be known that he might move the nation's capital and scheduled visit to Bytown. Tory supporters, including Mayor Robert Harvey, opposed having a reception for Lord Elgin. A meeting was organized by reform supporters of Elgin in what is still known as the Byward Market (a local pub claimed to be on the site of the riot). The two opposing sides clashed, first with sticks and stones but later with guns. Thirty persons were wounded, and one man, David Borthwick, was killed. Two days later, the two political factions, armed with artillery, rifles and pistols, faced off on the Sapper's bridge over the canal, and it seemed that more serious action would follow until the military arrived to diffuse the situation.

Lord Elgin cancelled his plans and did not come back to Bytown until 1853, just two years before Bytown was renamed Ottawa. Did Bytown's violence play a factor in the name change?

SMITH'S OVERVIEW IN 1846

By the time 1846 rolled around, Bytown was well enough established that it appears in Smith's Canadian Gazetteer, *published in Toronto that year; the section is reproduced word for word here.*

The District Town of the Dalhousie District is situated in the northeast corner of the township of Nepean, on the Ottawa River. It is divided into two portions called Upper and Lower Bytown; the former is the most aristocratic and the latter the most business portion of the town. The Lower Town has been long settled: the upper town has been more recently erected, and is situated about half a mile higher up the river, and on considerably higher ground. The land on which upper town is erected, together with a portion of that comprising the Lower Town, was purchased some years since for the sum of eighty pounds, and is now computed to be worth some 60,000 pounds. The Rideau Canal enters the Ottawa River just above the Lower Town, where eight handsome locks have been constructed to overcome the fall in the river.

The scenery about Bytown is, next to that at the Falls of Niagra [*sic*], the most picturesque of the inhabited portion of Canada. The Chaudière Falls, a short distance above the upper town, are very beautiful. Just below the falls, a handsome Suspension Bridge has been constructed over the Ottawa, which connects Upper with Lower Canada.

Bytown is principally supported by the lumber trade. On the Lower Canadian side of the river, slides have been constructed, to facilitate the passage of the rafts. Here all the timber brought down the river which has been cut on Crown lands, is measured, and the owner enters into a bond

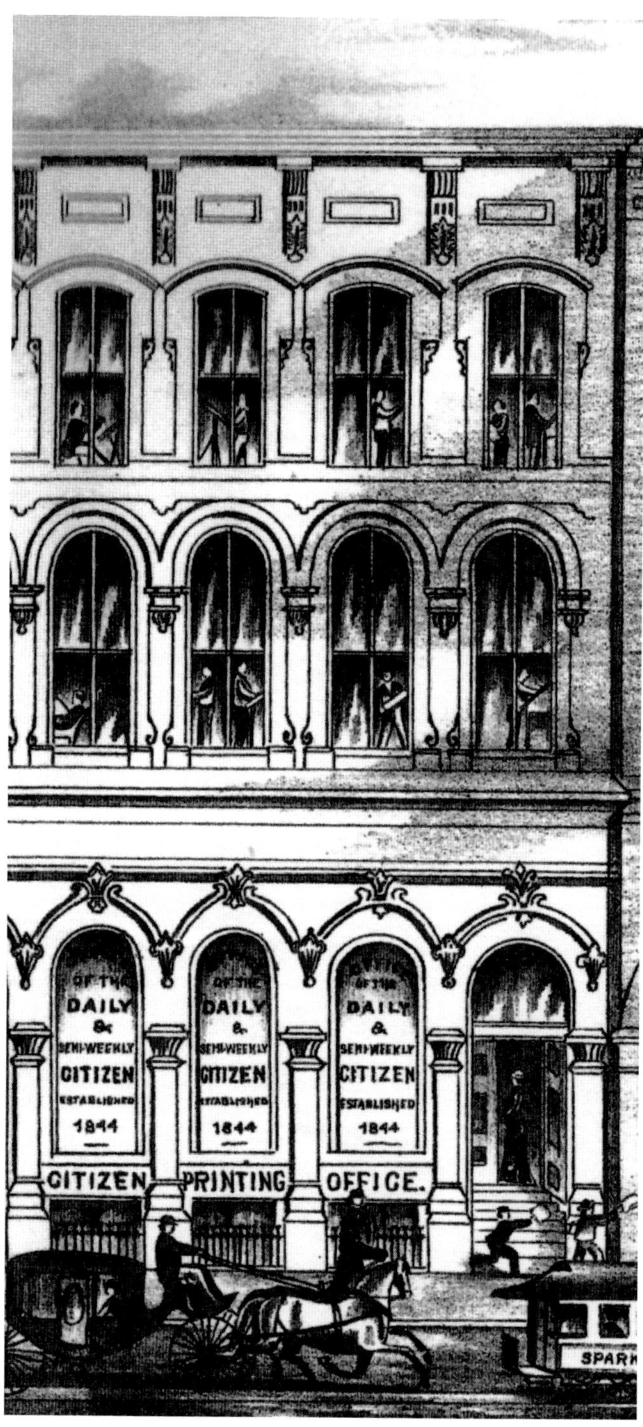

The first office of the *Ottawa Citizen*, a local newspaper that is still functioning today. *Belden.*

for the payment of the duties at Quebec. The town is fast improving in appearance and several handsome stone buildings are already erected. The Barracks are in a commanding situation, on the highest part of the bank of the river, between the upper and Lower Town, and are garrisoned by a company of Rifles.

The inhabitants of the Lower Town are about one-third French Canadians, the remainder are principally Irish.

Churches and chapels in the Lower Town, five; viz. Catholic, Free Church, two Methodist, and Baptist: in Upper Bytown, three, viz., Episcopal, Presbyterian, and Methodist. The Jail and Court House are of stone. Two Fire Engines are kept; one in the upper, and one in the Lower Town. There is a "Commercial Reading-room," supported by subscription; and a Mercantile Library Association.

A Fair is held at Bytown on the second Tuesday in April, and the third Wednesday in September. Three newspapers are published here weekly— the "Ottawa Advocate," "Bytown Gazette," and "Packet."

During the season, a steamboat plies daily between Bytown and Grenville, in Lower Canada, leaving Bytown in the morning, and returning from Grenville in the evening. And comfortable boats of a good size, ply on the Rideau Canal, between, Bytown and Kingston; but as they are generally engaged in towing barges, there is little dependence to be placed on the regularity; Population of Bytown, about 7,000. Post Office, Post daily; the mail is conveyed to Kingston on horseback. The following Government and District Offices are kept in Bytown: Judge of District Court, Sheriff, Clerk of Peace, Judge of Surrogate Court, Treasurer, Registrar of Surrogate Court, District Clerk, Clerk of District Court, Coroner, Collector of Timber Duties. Professions and Trades in Upper Bytown: three lawyers, two grist mills, two sawmills, three foundries, fourteen general stores, two lumber merchant stores, two druggists, one printer, five blacksmiths, two saddlers, seven shoe makers, four tailors, three cabinet makers, one tinsmith, one butcher, one baker, one barber, one wagon maker, four taverns, one ladies school, three bank agencies (Montreal, Upper Canada, bank of British North America). In Lower Bytown there was one physician and surgeon, four lawyers, thirty-two stores, six tanneries, two breweries, two druggists, one soap and candle factory, two printers, thirty-five taverns, fifty groceries, twenty beer shops, six saddlers, fourteen shoemakers, six tinsmiths, six tailors, three watchmakers, seven butchers, eight bakers, four cabinet makers, one coach maker, one turner, four wagon makers, two hatters, seven schools, two bank agencies (Commercial, and City Bank of Montreal).

J.R. BOOTH: THE OTTAWA LUMBER KING

Once the Rideau Canal was finished in 1832, Bytown had to find a new economic base. Surrounded by trees and with England crying out for lumber, it was only natural that the timber trade, in different phases, would become a staple of the new town situated on a major transportation route. One of the giants of the lumber business was John Rudolphus Booth, born in Waterloo, Quebec, who arrived in Ottawa in 1857 and lived here until his death on December 8, 1925.

There are many anecdotes about Booth and various idiosyncrasies, but one good, recent book is J.R. Trinnell's *J.R. Booth: The Life and Times of an Ottawa Lumber King*. It is a mixture of anecdotes and business statistics, as well as a chronological list of happenings in Booth's long life. In that life, Booth built and operated three railways in Ontario, was burned out a number of times but always rebuilt, married off one of his granddaughters to a Danish prince and lived almost ninety-nine years, outliving five of his eight children in the process.

Booth was known as a frugal man who didn't put on airs, despite his wealth and position. One anecdote concerns a particularly self-satisfied salesperson who came to meet Booth one morning for a business meeting. Spying a scruffy-looking individual standing outside the office, he offered him a dime to carry his sample case upstairs to Mr. Booth's office. The man obliged, and when asked where Mr. Booth was, he said, "You're looking at him. Where's my dime?" This is a story from my wife's grandfather, who knew Booth in the early part of the last century. Another well-known anecdote concerns the time Booth was criticized by a driver for giving only a ten-cent tip. The rationale was that Booth's son always gave a quarter. Booth replied gruffly, "That's alright. The boy has a rich father, but I was an orphan."

Booth came to the town now known as Ottawa in 1857, and many years later, shortly before his death, he was asked about his earliest memories of the town. He responded by commenting on the smell of the place. Thomas Anglin, a Montreal MP, also commented in *Hansard* (a report of the proceedings of the House of Commons) about the smell and dirt of "Our Town" in the early 1880s. One of my own recollections from when I first arrived in Ottawa in 1954 was the overwhelming smell of the pulp mills across the river early one April morning. While the closing of the pulp mills was an economic disaster for some, it did improve the air quality.

Before the famous fire of April 26, 1900, Booth lived at the corner of Wellington and Preston Streets, only a block or two from his mill. His neighbours on Wellington (also known as Richmond Road at the time) were the Salvation Army Rescue home and the Victoria Brewery. Farther up Wellington were a "lying-in" hospital, the residence of Mr. Frank Morgan and the Victoria Hotel. All were destroyed in the fire. Mr. Booth then built his home on Metcalfe Street near Somerset; it later became the Laurentian Club.

The big event of the 1924 social season was the wedding of Booth's granddaughter, Lois, to Prince Erik of Denmark. They were married at All Saints Anglican Church in Sandy Hill, and Deputy Chief of Police Gilhooly said, "Yesterday afternoon every available man was pressed into service, but ten men could not handle a crowd of ten thousand, ninety percent of them were woman who would not do as they were told but smiled and giggled the whole time," according to the February 12, 1924 *Ottawa Journal*. J.R. Booth did not attend the wedding. There was no fairy tale ending to the wedding either. The couple had two children, but Prince Erik arranged an annulment of the wedding because of a friendship between Lois and Thorkeld Julesberg, the prince's secretary. Lois married Julesberg after the annulment but died in Denmark in 1941. Her body was transported back to Canada, and she was buried at Beechwood Cemetery. Her father's home was at 285 Charlotte Street, and it was eventually sold to the Soviet government for its embassy. The old building burned down on January 1, 1956, because the embassy staff refused to allow Ottawa firefighters access to "Soviet territory." So ended one of the interesting stories about Ottawa history, of a "poor boy" who made good and whose money was able to advance his family to the highest levels of society. On the day after the wedding, the bride's father joked that he was naming himself the "Count de Cost" because of the price tag on the proceedings.

After his death in December 1925, at his request, J.R. Booth was buried in a relatively simple ceremony, but crowds still lined the street to honour the "old man of the lumber industry."

Lumbermen and the Timber Industry

Even before the Rideau Canal was built, there was a timber industry in the region. In 1800, Philemon Wright settled across the Ottawa River in what is now Quebec. He built a mill and processed an abundant supply of timber. In 1806, he and his son put together the first square timber raft and took it downriver to Quebec City via the Ottawa and St. Lawrence Rivers. The fur trade was declining, and the timber trade was waiting to take its place. The first settlers engaged in lumbering during the winter as a kind of cash crop to supplement farming. European events gave a great boost to the trade, and this boost led to the first wave of immigration.

From 1793 to 1815, Britain's economy was heavily focused on its war with France. The war ended with Napoleon's defeat, but the Ottawa Valley timber trade was well established. British merchants were established in Quebec City in 1803. Philemon Wright is seen as the father of the Ottawa Valley timber trade. Under his leadership, trees were chopped down to make space for agricultural development. Much wood was used regionally for heating or to build houses, barns or infrastructure. However, because of the European developments, "timbering" became part of the seasonal economic cycle of the Ottawa Valley settlers and a welcome supplement to subsistence-based farming.

The timber industry depended on the success of several different components: the river men, the log drive, the timber rafts and the infrastructure related to logging. There were fellers, sawyers, skidders, teamsters, river drivers and the "bull of the woods," who was the walking boss or the overall foreman. They all had their own skills and talents and, in the old folk songs, their own stories to tell. Speaking of stories, there are literally hundreds of stories from the camps. One of my favourites, told to me by my wife's grandfather, was the one about the "blood charm." It was a danger of the trade that bad cuts would happen, and everyone was a long way from medical help. Certain men were said to have had the ability to stop blood flow simply by laying their hands on the victim. This might be an exaggeration, for "the timber beasts" were fond of tall tales. Nearly all the stories, though, had elements of truth in them. It was said that some axe men's skill was such that one could drive a stake into the ground some thirty feet from a tree he was about to fell and hit the stake with the falling trunk. A dozen different things could have influenced its fall. Donald McKay's book has one lumberjack describing a white pine as

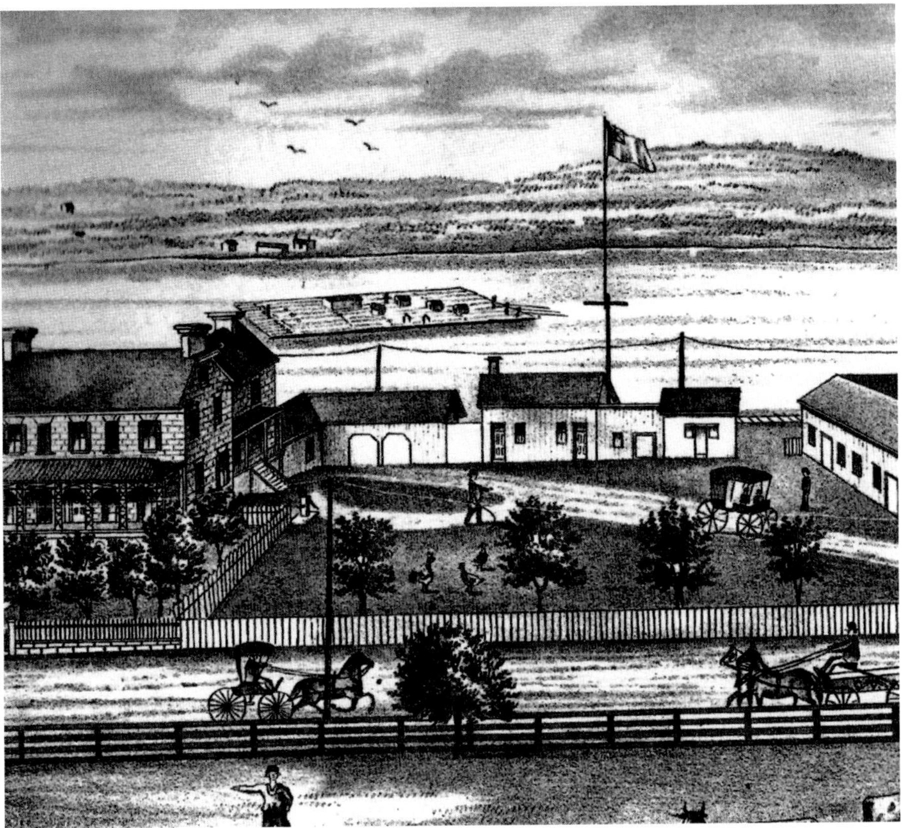

Timber raft on river. *Belden.*

follows: "Its trunk was as straight and handsomely grown as a moulded candle and measured six feet in diameter. In length it was one hundred and forty feet, about sixty-five feet of it was free from limbs, and retained its diameter remarkably well."

The "fellers" lived in bunkhouses in the woods and worked a six-day week. They stopped work early on Saturdays and rested from their labours on Sundays. The "skidders" took over once the trees had been reduced to logs or squared off—depending on the market for which they were destined. Sometimes as many as twenty-two pairs of workhorses were linked together to haul the wood out of the bush. It took men with great horse skills and an understanding of the animals to manage such a train. Once the logs were deposited on the shores of the Ottawa or one of its major tributaries, another group of workmen took over. These

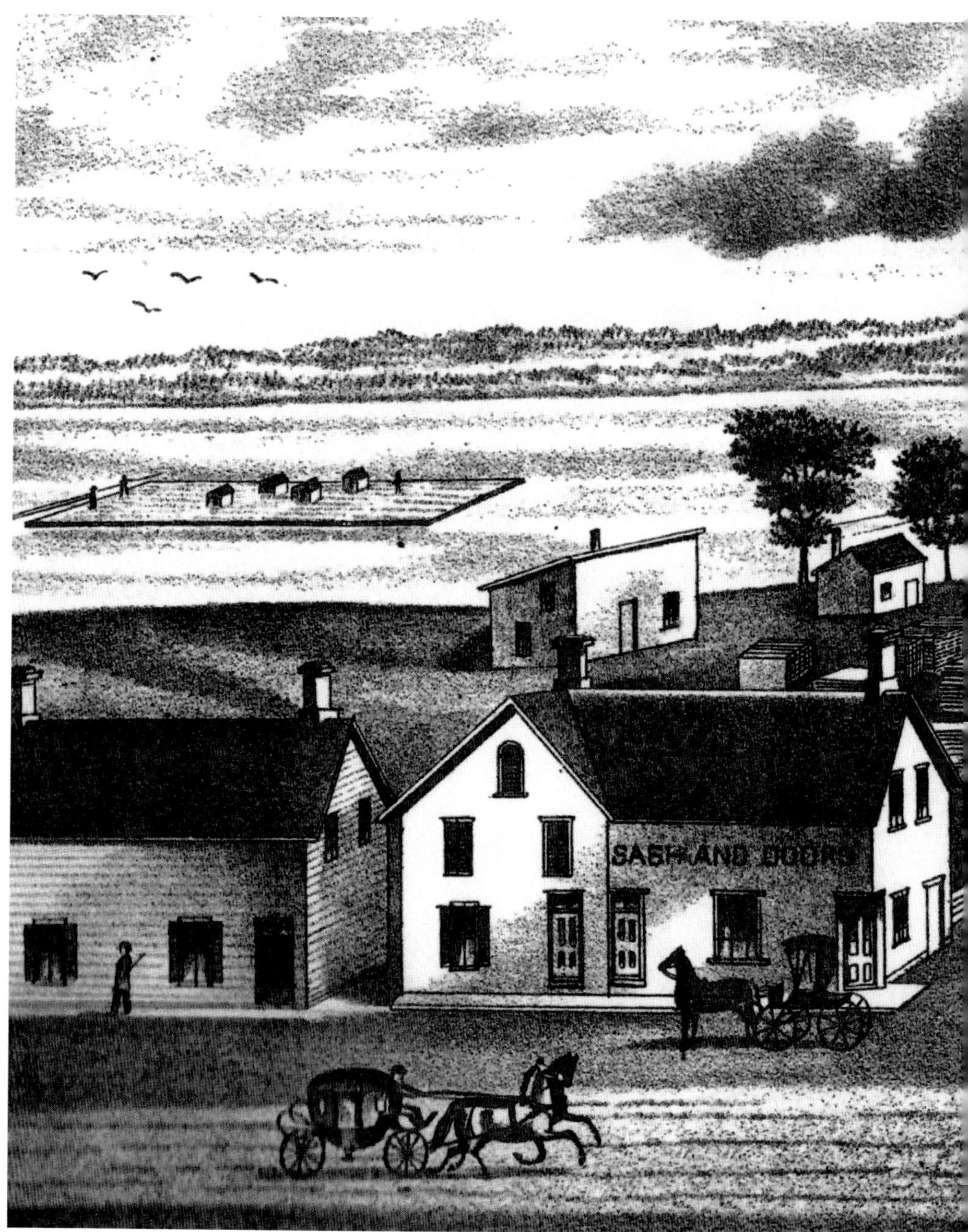

A sawmill on the banks of the Ottawa River. *Belden.*

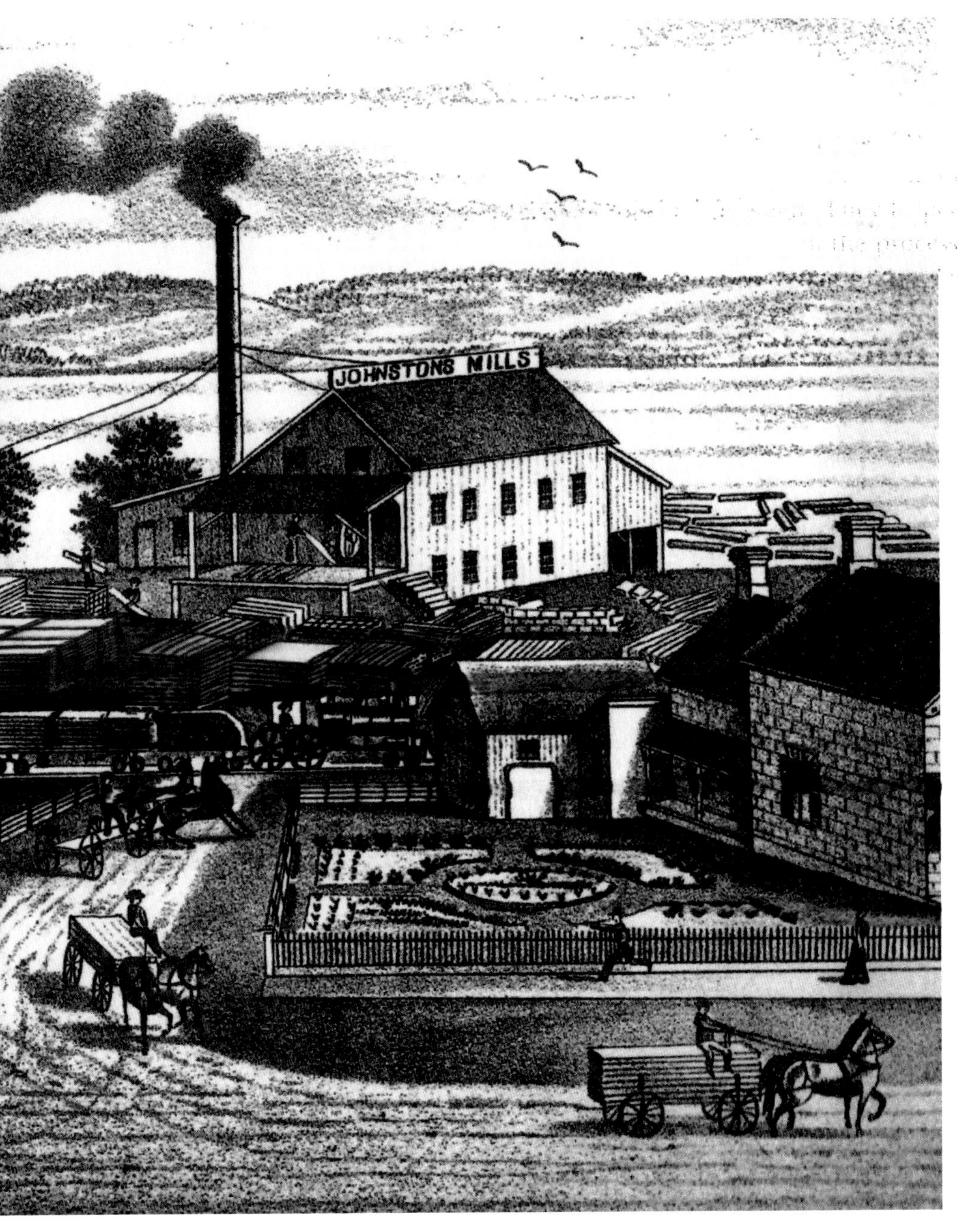
JOHNSTONS MILLS

were the river drivers whose job it was to get the logs to where they could be assembled into rafts. Even today, some of those logs are still salvaged from the bottom of the rivers they travelled and fetch a good price on the markets.

The river driving took place in the spring and became the stuff of legends. The drivers herded loose logs, unlike the raftsmen. They leaped from log to log to break up jams and took enormous risks in the process. At rapids, there was always a problem getting the logs past, until Ruggles Wright designed the first timber slide in 1829, which allowed the logs to continue downriver. They were in use for more than a century, and the Prince of Wales even took a well-protected trip down one of the timber slides in 1860. Rafts were unusual, ungainly craft containing living and sleeping quarters for their passengers. They were made up of "cribs," or segments that could be many metres across. Trips from the woods to the markets could take many months. Once the Rideau Canal was completed, timber would be shipped to inland Canadian markets. The river men became internationally known, and about three hundred accompanied a relief expedition down the Nile River to relieve General Gordon at Khartoum, as per Robert Leggett's seminal work.

The lumbermen lived interesting lives both in their camps and when they went to town. In the camps, the men would sleep in a large cabin built of round logs that was furnished with bunk beds and a large table with chairs for the meals. A fire burned continually in a sand pit. Typical fare included beans, lard, flour and pork meat. They spent their Saturday nights fiddling, dancing, singing and telling tall stories. They could sleep in on Sunday mornings. A lively mix of both music and storytelling styles was created due to the wide variety in the men's backgrounds. Many songs, in both French and English, mentioned the names of real people and events from the time.

A book from 1895 titled *Up to Date or the Life of a Lumberman* describes the lifestyle on a Sunday: "Sunday is cleaning up day, the men doing their washing and mending on that day (that is the few who would go to that trouble). Quite a number would never change their underclothes or shirts until the clothes wore out and as to washing their feet, such a thing never entered their minds."

The lumbermen developed a reputation for being rough and sometimes troublesome. Upon their return to Ottawa, these men often became quite rowdy, and brawls would ensue; damage to public property was quite common. Loggers often easily handed over much of their winter earnings to

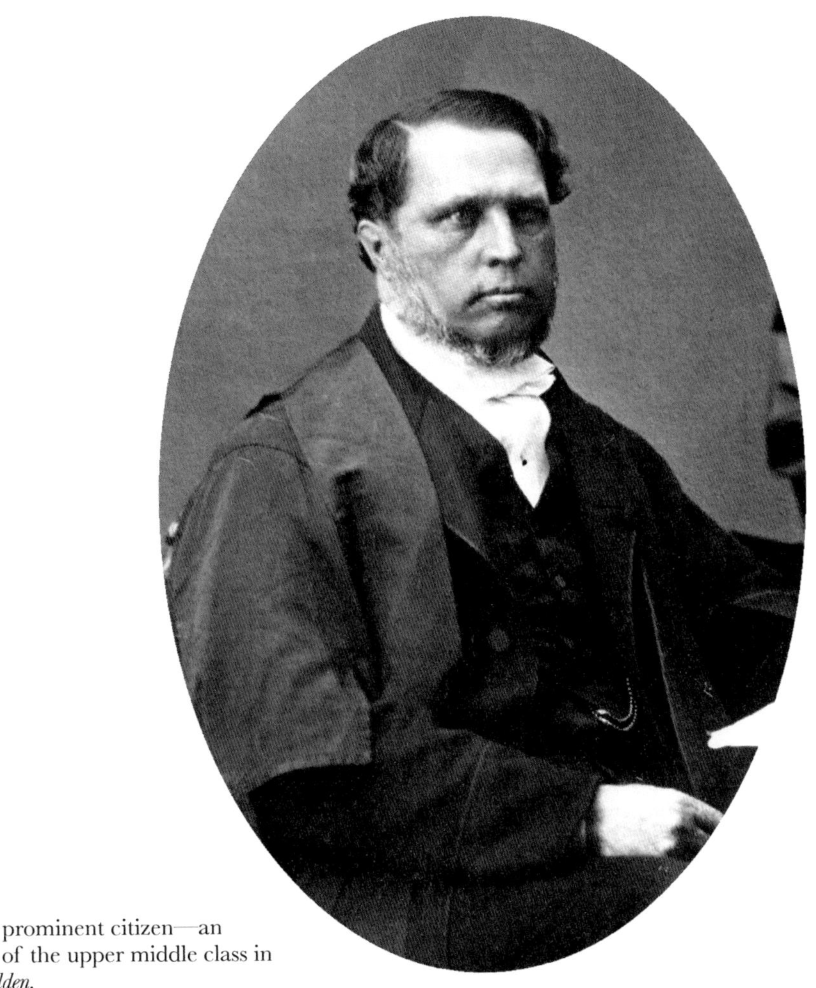

An early prominent citizen—an example of the upper middle class in 1879. *Belden.*

merchants, bookkeepers and others shortly after their return to town. Ottawa citizens might not have liked the behavior, but they knew that lumbering was the lifeblood of the community so they probably turned a blind eye to most of the activity.

Before leaving the life of the lumberman, it is illuminating to review the detailed purchases of a lumberjack coming out of the woods. In his book *The Lumberjacks*, Donald MacKay gives us a fine account. The following is a summary of the expenditures of one Mr. Baptiste Fortin in spending $96.50 of his $150.00 winter wages:

Drinks and tobacco with friends	*$30.00*
Whiskey, pipe and earrings	*$4.25*
Breakfast of Oysters	*$1.50*
Hair care (cut and dyed)	*$5.50*
One photo (25 copies made)	*$5.00*
Sightseeing on horse and buggy	*$7.00*
One suit	*$17.00*
Boots	*$5.00*
Watch and Ring	*$3.75*
Room and Board	*$5.00*
Tips to seamstress and organ grinders	*$4.00*
Stitches after a fight	*$1.00*
Lost a bet	*$2.00*
Cab to the railway station	*$1.50*
Train ticket home	*$4.00*

The balance he turned over to his wife, who was probably horrified he had so little to show for his six months of work in the woods. Baptiste probably never heard the end of it. Two-thirds of a winter's work blown in a few days was a little extreme! Let's leave the loggers with that tale of Baptiste "blowin her in," as a trip to the city was called. They worked hard and played hard and left us a legacy of economic returns, stories and shanty songs that we should long remember. Readers who wish to learn more about the life and times of the lumbermen are invited to consult any of the sources mentioned in this admittedly short summary.

Songs and Poems of the "Timberbeasts"

The Shantyboy's Song (circa 1840s)

The choppers and the sawyers,
They lay the timber low,
The swampers and the skidders,
They haul it to and fro.

At four o'clock each morning,
The boss begins to shout,
"Heave out my jolly teamsters,
It's time to start the route."

The teamsters they all jump up,
In a most fretful way,
"Where is me boots? Where is me pants?
Me socks is gone astray."

Peter Emberley from Prince Edward Island was a young man who was crushed by rolling logs near Boiestown, New Brunswick, in 1882. A man named John Calhoun, who was his workmate, carried the dying young man to a nearby farm, and as he passed away, he spoke deliriously of his home and his family. The man who carried him wrote a song, which became one of the best-loved ballads on the river:

I hired to work in the lumber woods,
Where they cut the tall spruce down,
While loading sleds with yarded logs,
I received my own death wound…
Adieu unto my dearest friend

I mean my mother dear,
She raised a son who fell as soon,
As he left her tender care…

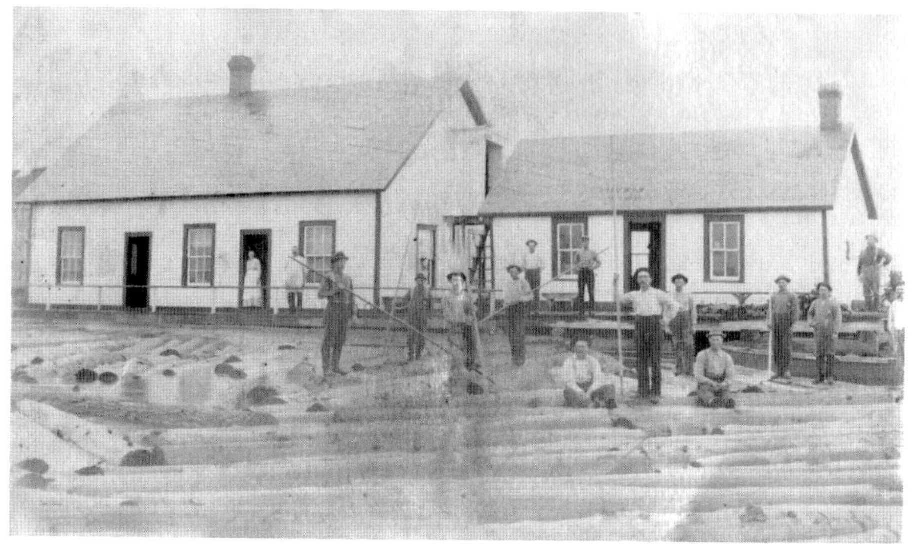

Homes for timber workers in the marsh area. *MacKay.*

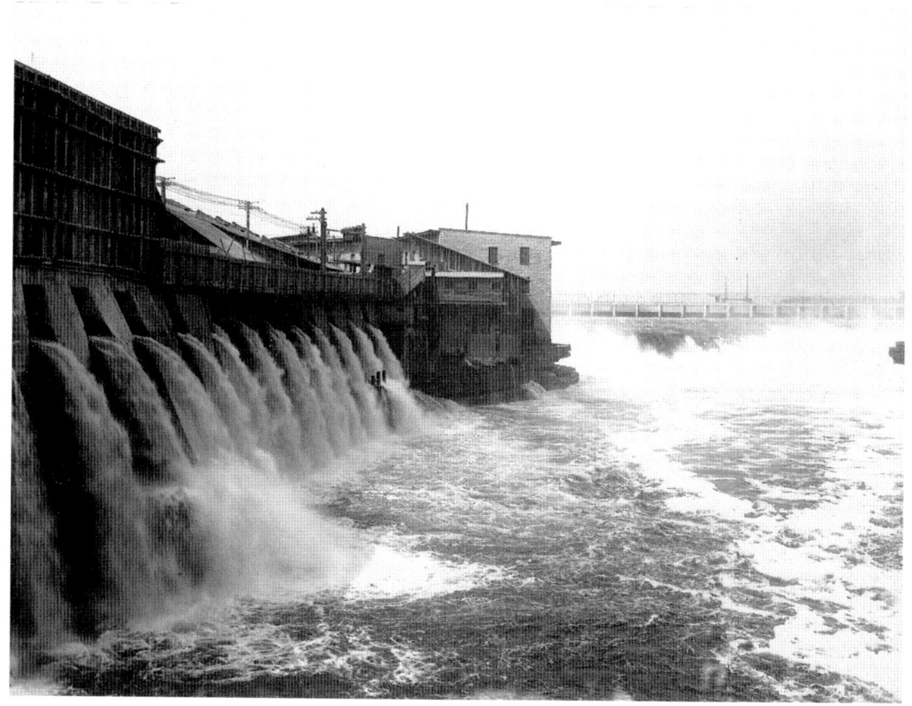

A falls to overcome on the river. *Ottawa City Archives.*

Following was a tune that illustrated the dangers of the trade:

The Jam on Gerry's Rocks (Traditional)

Come all ye jolly river boys,
I'll have ye all draw near
And listen to the dangers,
Which ye will quickly hear.

There were many drownings, and accidental deaths were not an uncommon thing as a result of this difficult job. Sad songs were written to retell the river tragedies. For instance, a ballad was written describing the drowning of a young man named Anthony Barrett of Belleville, Ontario, on June 2, 1860:

"Twas on the Napanee" they sang "while driving sawlogs down.
He fell into the water there, and there alas, was drowned…"

A man named Jimmy Judd was drowned on the Bonnechere;
He went forth to break the jam, and
With it he went through,
In spite of his activity,
His precious life to save,
In vain was his exertion, for he met his watery grave.

In 1878, Jimmy Phalen lost his life trying to carry out his forman's orders. As he tried to break the jam, two rafts collided, and he fell in. It took an hour to find his body in the current:

Now here, now there, his body went, a-tumbling o'er and o'er
One fearful cry for Mercy,
"O Lord look down on me,"
His soul got free from early care,
Gone to Eternity.

The lumberjacks, while in their shanties, thought about food, talked about food and even dreamed about food. Sometimes they would manage to shoot some game on Sundays, but fresh food was rare. An old Ottawa Valley song, "The Chapeau Boys," tells of the extent to which life was about food. A few lumbermen wrote a song about a dinner they ate on a farm on their way to log Black River:

We had roast beef and mutton and good apple pie,
Good bread, fresh butter which could make you surprise,
We had cookies, rice pudding, our tea sweet and strong,
And good early carrots, full six inches long,
We had good cucumbers and cabbage, boiled and raw,
And the leg of a beaver Bob stole from a squaw.

Lumberjack's Prayer

I pray dear Lord, for Jesus' sake,
Give us this day a T-bone steak;
Hallowed be Thy Name,
But don't forget to send the same.

The above was part of a "Wobbly" logging song brought into British Columbia before World War I.

At some camps, the supplies for the year arrived via the riverbeds. Supplies would be boated right up the shallow riverbeds on seventy-foot scows that could carry five tons. If the water became deep, the towline would be let out, and then horses did their pulling from paths on the banks. However, at most camps, the men had to take to portaging to get the supplies to the tougher areas. This had to be done in the winter and early spring. In northern Ontario, one teamster might drive three sleighs, and he would be covered in frost and rendered unrecognizable from exposure to the bitter winds. Portage men were famous as they came through the villages parading their strong horses and caravan of goods down the road. Sometimes portage men had to trudge alongside the sleighs to keep them from tipping, and there is a tale told of when a man name Ernie McQuaid was soaked by a hogshead being smashed as the team jolted forwards. The temperatures made this unfortunate incident a dangerous one in the thirty-below weather. His friend, who was a renowned jokester, jumped from the sleigh and in most colourful verse recited the following prayer:

Dear Lord of Hosts and Holy Ghosts
And our Sweet Redeeming Jesus
Come to our aid and save McQuaid
Before the bastard freezes.

In a pulpwood camp after supper, the men would sing, dance, smoke and talk about their families and the week's work. Anyone who could sing well or even play the spoons or a mouth organ would be highly prized. Songs and poems were written, sung and passed on over the decades. Often the songs and ballads they composed would poke fun at themselves. Here is a small taste of some of those remembered.

The Maid from Tidehead
From the Bay of Chaleur, New Brunswick

In the dark, tangled forest where lumberjacks sing,
And their saws and their axes, the music will ring
Oh the nights they are weary and the days they are long
But my comrades they cheer me with music and song.

Their nights are oft in gambling passed
And some will win tobacco fast
And then like Satan they will cheat
And swear at cards, they can't be beat,
Out in the dark they dare not stray,
For fear old Nick takes them away.

A man named Gorman could compose a thirty-two-verse song and sing it on the spot, including one he wrote about himself:

And when they see me coming
Their eyes stick out like prongs,
Saying, "Beware of Larry Gorman
He's the man who makes the songs."

As this chapter comes to an end, I will leave you with a Sunday menu from one of the better lumber camps in 1935. Company-run camps fed their men well, as they worked up quite an appetite:

Breakfast
Oatmeal—stewed prunes
Pork and beans—bologna—toast
Raisin pie—ginger cake
Bread—butter—sugar—molasses
Tea—coffee—cheese

Dinner
Pea soup—pot roast—mash potatoes—mustard—pickled onions
Steamed rice pudding—nutmeg sauce—blancmange—pie
Bread—butter—sugar—syrup
Tea—milk—sugar—cheese

Supper
Pea soup
Beef—cold salt pork—mustard
Sugar pie—raisin pie—molasses cookies
Bread—butter—molasses
Tea—milk—sugar—cheese

Part IV
The Growth of Ottawa

Bytown Becomes Ottawa

There seems no better way to describe this topic than to paraphrase and quote Robert Leggett's work on the "Rideau Waterway" first published in 1965 (though the quote is from the 1972 edition): "Bytown's maturity came fully into public view when, on February 8, 1853 a petition was presented to the Executive Council praying that the name of the town be changed to Ottawa and that the status of the city is given to the settlement."

Although this initial request was not granted, a subsequent one was. The necessary legislation was passed in Quebec City, and on January 1, 1855, the name of Bytown disappeared and was replaced by Ottawa. The modern city was born. Not long afterwards, because of the competition between Montreal, Toronto and Kingston, Queen Victoria decided that the lumber town should become the capital city of Canada. It was decreed that Ottawa was to be the official capital of Upper and Lower Canada. This continued after Confederation, as Canada became one nation on July 1, 1867.

Ottawa was fortunate in hiring some prominent supporters for making it the capital. Lady Head, the wife of the governor, loved the beauty of Bytown so much that she lobbied on its behalf and drew a sketch that she sent to Queen Victoria. Her husband, Sir Edmund Head, sent a confidential dispatch recommending Ottawa because it was some distance from the American border. Memories of quick invasions from the United States during 1812–14 were still fresh in the minds of all involved. He also argued that the Rideau Canal would further justify its expense if Ottawa were chosen as the capital.

Whatever the various influences were, Queen Victoria chose Ottawa, and it has remained the capital to this day.

MEDICINE COMES TO BYTOWN

I was asked recently how only one doctor and pharmacist mentioned in Smith's 1846 summary could possibly have provided healthcare to a town of seven thousand souls. The truth is that there were other sources of medical help, although why Smith did not mention them is a good question.

Recently, the Historical Society of Ottawa published a paper of the latest winner of the Colonel By Award for local history (Mike Nelles of Carleton University), and it is an excellent source of information on early medical care and a good bibliography of sources on the subject. The Bytown pamphlet series is available through the historical society and is also available at the National Library of Canada and the Ottawa Public Library.

The first medical facility in Ottawa was a twenty-bed military hospital established by John By in 1826 on Barracks Hill where the West Block now stands. The hospital operated for fifty years. It was available to the civilian population only in dire emergencies, such as outbreaks of malaria, typhus and cholera. These kinds of outbreaks occurred in 1827, 1832 and 1847. The Sisters of Charity, under the capable leadership of Sister (later Mother Superior) Elizabeth Bruyere, opened the first civilian general hospital in 1845. (It is curious that this was not mentioned in Smith's 1846 *Gazetteer*.)

In 1903, a memoir of the early days of Bytown medicine was written by Dr. Beaumont Small, who recalled the days when doctors rode around the settlements dispensing care to the settlers. A more recent account of the early days was written in 1993 by Linda Tresham as part of the Bytown pamphlet series. Tresham documented the great cholera epidemic of 1832. Both authors decried the lack of interest and attention given to medical care at the time.

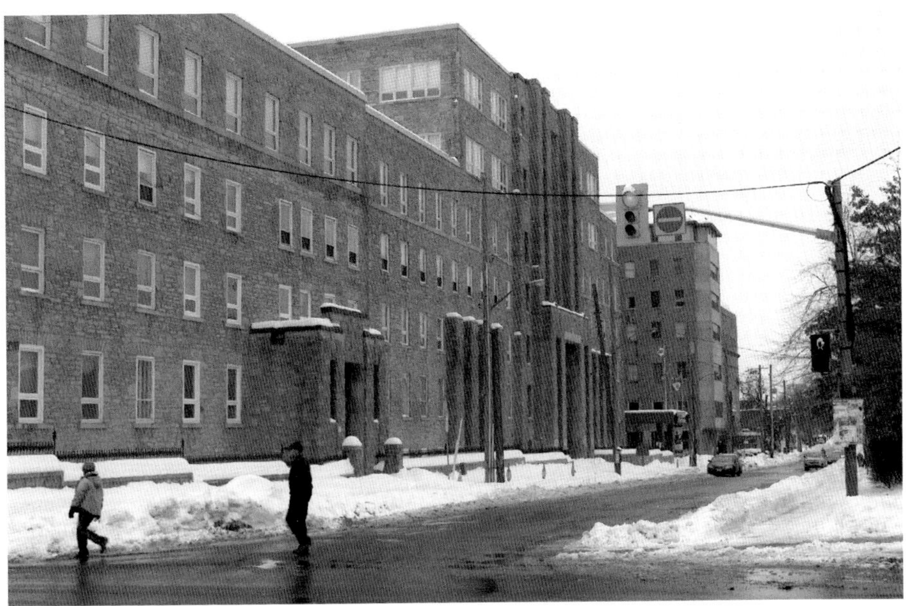

Bruyere Hospital, site of the first public hospital in Ottawa.

The earliest recorded doctor in Bytown was Dr. A.J. Christie, who became a prominent advocate for medical care. In 1836, he also founded the first newspaper in Bytown, the *Bytown Gazette*. Christie first came to Bytown in 1827 as a military doctor for Rideau Canal workers. He was one of the few doctors to remain here after the completion of the canal in 1832. There is some debate over his medical training, but he appears to have served the population until his death in 1843. In those days, according to Charles Roland in *Ontario Medicine* (1983), doctors were paid in such things as "chickens, eggs, home brew, a slab of bacon or chores." The real "driver" of improved medical care in the town was a series of epidemics that threatened the population. The worst of these was the cholera epidemic of 1832, which is deserving of an entire section itself.

In June 1832, Lieutenant Governor Colborne authorized the first board of health in Bytown under the chairmanship of Dr. Christie. One of its first acts was to close all schools and public buildings to prevent the spread of disease. A temporary wooden hospital was constructed on what is now the site of the Royal Canadian Mint. It was the first medical facility constructed for the benefit of the civilian population. Within one month, fifteen to thirty-five cholera patients had died—an indication of the mortality of cholera in those days. Also, the lack of medical knowledge of the time probably contributed greatly to the death rate in 1832. The hospital was eventually scrapped in 1834 and sold as firewood.

In 1844, it was clear that the military hospital was inadequate for a town growing with the lumber industry. In February 1845, a group of nuns arrived by sleigh led by the twenty-seven-year-old Sister Bruyere. The Sisters took up visiting the sick and opened a seven-bed hospital in the spring. Within a year, the facility had become inadequate, and a petition was signed for a land grant to build a larger facility. Of the signers of the petition, only four were Roman Catholic, an indication that the need for a bigger hospital was broadly felt among the population. Fourteen lots were provided, and plans went ahead for construction of a hospital that stood on the same ground later occupied by the old General Hospital, which was eventually renamed and is now operated by the Sisters as the Bruyere Centre. The town was immediately challenged with the great typhus epidemic of 1847–48. This was brought to Ottawa by unfortunate immigrants who died in great numbers on the trip to Canada and even after they arrived. The bulk of the survivors were Irish immigrants fleeing the potato famine in Ireland.

Following the example of the Catholic General Hospital, approval was granted in 1847 for the construction of a Protestant General Hospital. While medical care was still chancy at best, the foundation had been laid for the proper medical treatment of citizens. The first permanent health board was created in 1851, and the first stone hospital was erected on the northwest corner of Rideau and Wurtemburg Street. From these early beginnings grew the excellent if sometimes crowded medical services we enjoy today.

Mechanic's Institutes: Education Comes to Ottawa

Not very many people in early Ottawa had the educational advantages of today's society; many wished for it but had to leave school, where it existed, as soon as they were of money-earning age. Those who could afford a classical or technical education tended to be those whose parents had already had some measure of success. Technical knowledge came through apprenticeship and on-the-job learning. Women and girls were almost excluded from the education systems that did exist. However, a good portion of those already educated believed that all persons were educable and that educating was the key to a better society both socially and economically.

In the early 1820s, organizations called Mechanic's Institutes were established in Great Britain and the United States. These groups were dedicated to "improving the mind of the working class." In Bytown in the 1840s, several attempts were made to establish similar institutions, but final success did not come until 1853. The institutes were aimed at factory workers but were more used by clerks and shop assistants. After the twelve- to fourteen-hour days of the times, most factory workers preferred relaxing in the local pub with their buddies.

On January 28, 1847, there was a meeting of prominent citizens in the Oddfellow's Hall to create a Bytown Mechanic's Institute. Despite their best efforts at fundraising and the purchase of a collection of books, the institute became defunct in 1849. The organizers persisted, however. They wanted to show that Bytown was progressive. In early 1853, a provisional committee with the strong support of Robert Bell, publisher of the *Ottawa Citizen*, was struck to start a "Bytown Mechanic's Institute and Athenaeum."

A Province of Canada Act was passed in 1853, establishing the Mechanic's Institute in Bytown. Fees were set at five dollars per annum, a sum that could represent as much as one week's salary for a working man. This might have been a factor in the later history of the institute.

The highest point of institute membership was 438 in 1866–67. At a general meeting in 1867, a recorded vote of 109 attendees showed the following mix: 13 professionals, 16 merchants, 12 civil servants, 3 lumber merchants, 16 in service industries, 10 bookkeepers and clerks, 1 farmer, 4 labourers, 2 servants, 2 gentlemen and 20 for whom no occupation was given. This would be hardly representative of the working class. The organization apparently died in 1907 as professional societies, museums and public libraries proliferated in Ottawa.

In 1902, the president of the institute still felt the society's activities were useful, but the handwriting was on the wall with the opening of the Carnegie public library in 1906. In November 1906, the president, Dr. Otto Klotz, still promoted the work of the institute but also stated that "the great mass of the people is not hungering for the intellectual development but is rather in search of amusement entertainment and forms of diversion as involve little or no mental effort."

R. Forbes Hirsch, who researched the history of Mechanic's Institutes, offered the following comments in a 1991 publication: "It cannot be said that the Institute suffered from competition in its early days for the limited

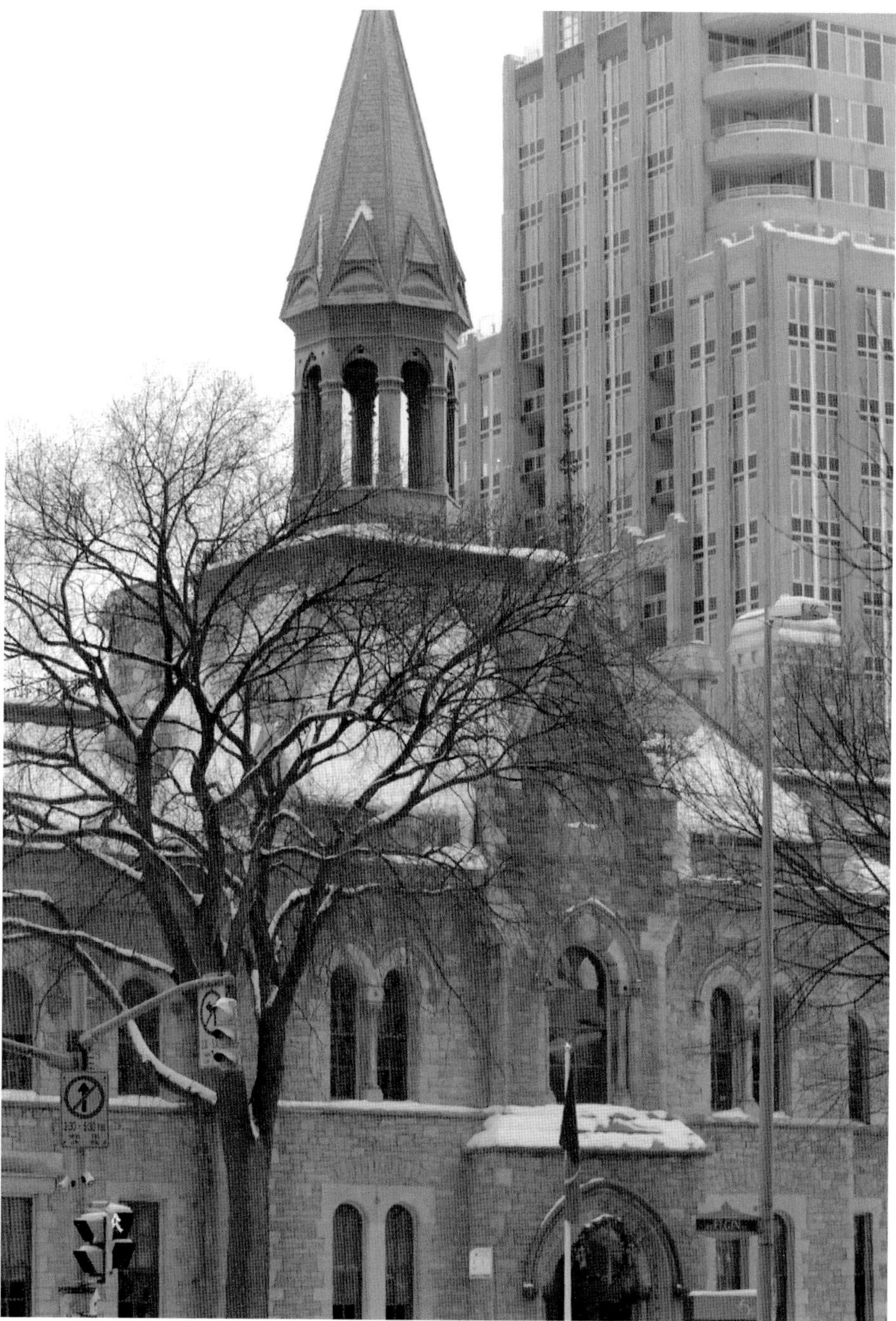

The original teacher's college—now part of city hall.

leisure time of the residents they hoped to attract—the only competition were the pubs, worship services and other church activities." Hirsch felt that what had really evolved was a social club where the lecture topics were of more interest to better-educated middle- and upper-class citizens.

For workers who put in long hours by today's standards and who really couldn't afford the fees charged, the idea was great, but the implementation suffered from many problems.

Science Comes to Ottawa

The city of Ottawa has been from its very beginnings, and is still today, a major centre of scientific thinking, research and technological transfer and development in Canada. The Rideau Canal, which was the principal catalyst in the creation of the town that became Ottawa, was a technological marvel of its time. From only a few houses in 1826 to a town of 1,500 in 1832 and a larger town of 7,000 in 1846, growth after the canal was constructed was constant.

In 1831, the Englishman Cartermale's writing about the area stressed its advantages. But in that era, science had not yet established itself as a major economic force and a technological catalyst. That would take another century. In fact, the first scientific establishment in Ottawa would take another fifty years, but it would soon be followed by others as the usefulness of scientific assistance in resource industries became more established.

The Geological Survey of Canada (GSC) was formed in 1842 in conjunction with McGill University in Montreal under the leadership of Sir William Logan; it remained there until there was a change in government. It caught international attention in 1851 at the great exhibition in London, England. A decision was made by the McKenzie government to move the GSC to Ottawa in 1880. Montreal interests were outraged. They threatened the governor-general with litigation unless the decision taken by Parliament was reversed. Logan had died in 1875, and the executors of his estate claimed that his museum was inextricably linked to the GSC and that the move was, therefore, an illegal expropriation.

Hansard reported the comments of Thomas Anglin, MP, on the decision to move the GSC: "The building [referring to the museum, which housed the survey] looks out on what? On a cart stand, a pile of filth, with a stench

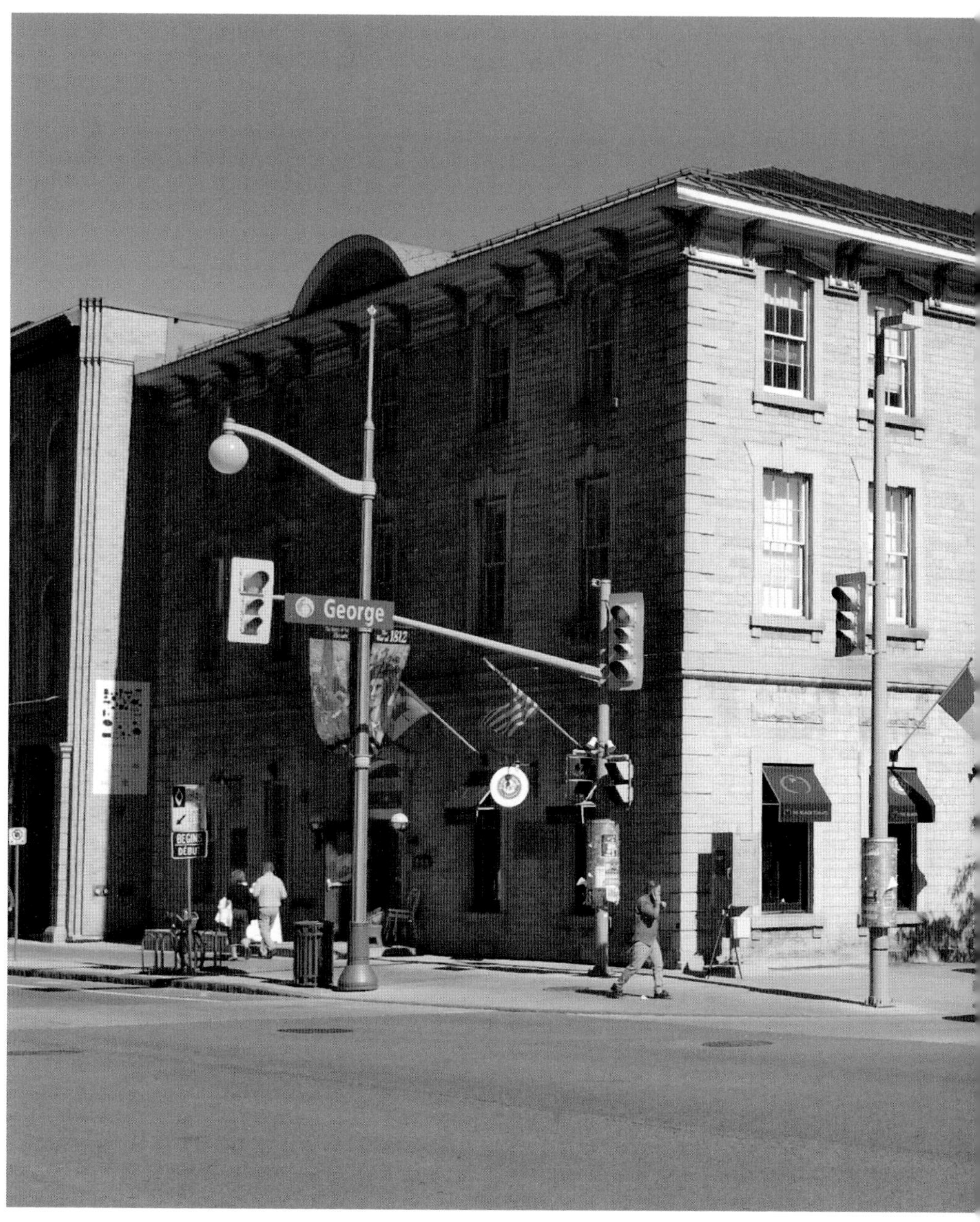

The first home of the geological survey and the hotel featured in the great hotel scandal, 1838.

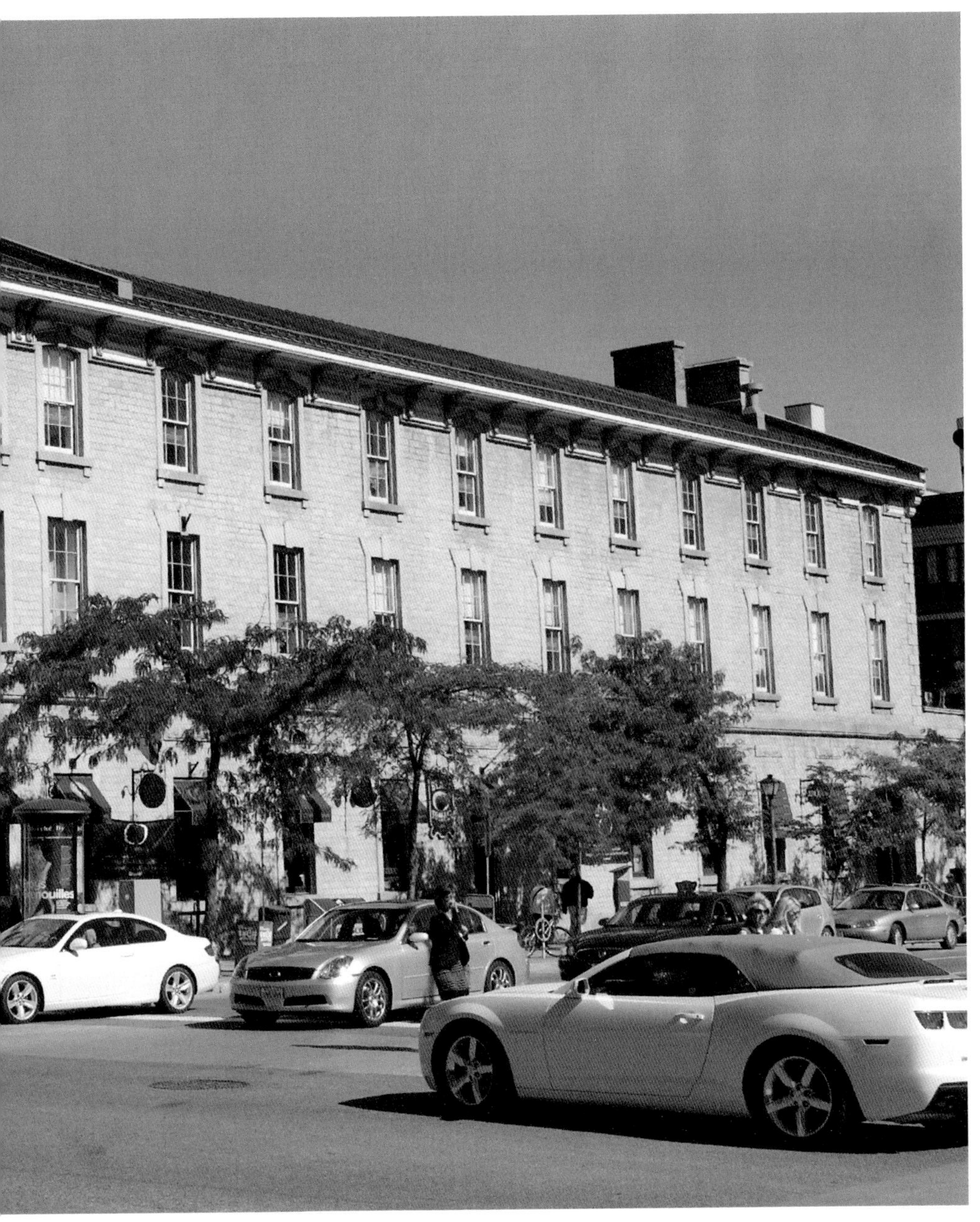

pervading the atmosphere all the time, with dust in summer and mud in all the other seasons."Anglin was referring to the building at the corner of George and Sussex Drive in Ottawa that had previously served as a hotel. Alfred R.C. Selwyn, who had replaced Logan in 1869, was at first against the move but later admitted that the change had been a good one when he compared visitor statistics between Montreal and Ottawa. Visitors in Ottawa exceeded those in Montreal by a wide margin.

Despite the threats and environmental criticisms, the GSC moved to Ottawa as planned and has remained there ever since. Not long thereafter, agricultural science became centred here, followed by astronomy and fisheries. In 1882, the scientific section of the Royal Society of Canada was established in Ottawa, and a majority of local scientists became charter members. By 1920, the National Research Council had been established, and it got its own laboratories in 1933. Ottawa still has a reputation as a leader in scientific research in new fields, such as computer technology and medicine.

The Central Experimental Farm

Where else in the world do you have a 1,200-acre farm in the centre of the nation's capital city? Here, where land was and is plentiful, we have such a monument to science and history. The Central Experimental Farm (CEF) was created in 1886, recommended by George Saunders and approved by Minister of Agriculture Sir John Carling. It is now a historic site—a beautiful place of broad fields, shade trees, the National Arboretum, an animal barn and picnic sites. In the winter, the hills are used for sledding and tobogganing.

Here was the development of marquis wheat by Sir Charles Saunders about 1910 and the development of canola during and after World War II. Hundreds of other scientific studies have benefitted the economy and brought fame to those who produced them. On the centenary anniversary of the farm, Dr. Thomas Anstey authored a work entitled *One Hundred Harvests* that has proven invaluable on the beginnings of the Central Experimental Farm and the network of experimental farms across the nation.

It all began with—what else for Canada—a Commission of Inquiry. As the country expanded westward in the nineteenth century, increasing pressure was felt by the government to provide agricultural advice on crops, the care

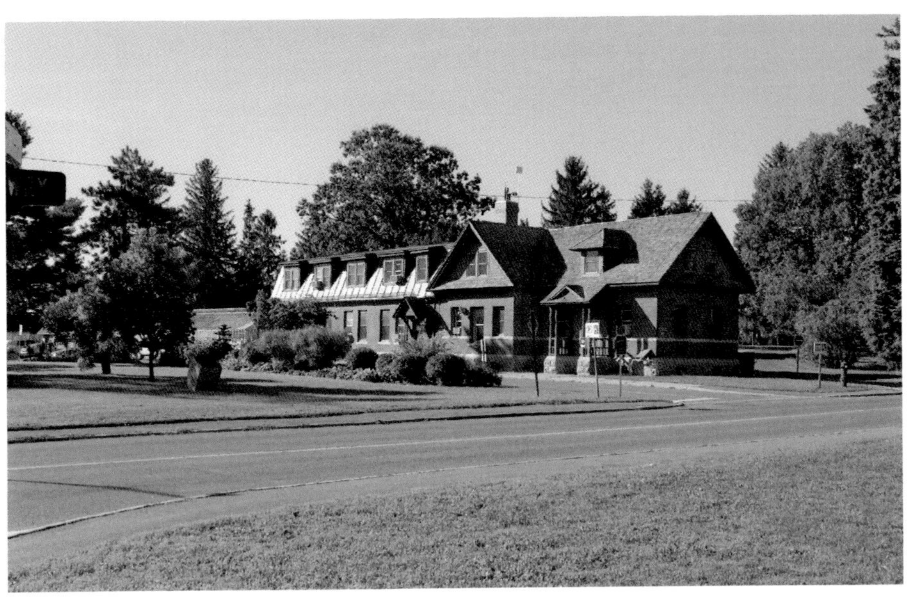

Building #75 at the Central Experimental Farm. Marquis wheat was developed here.

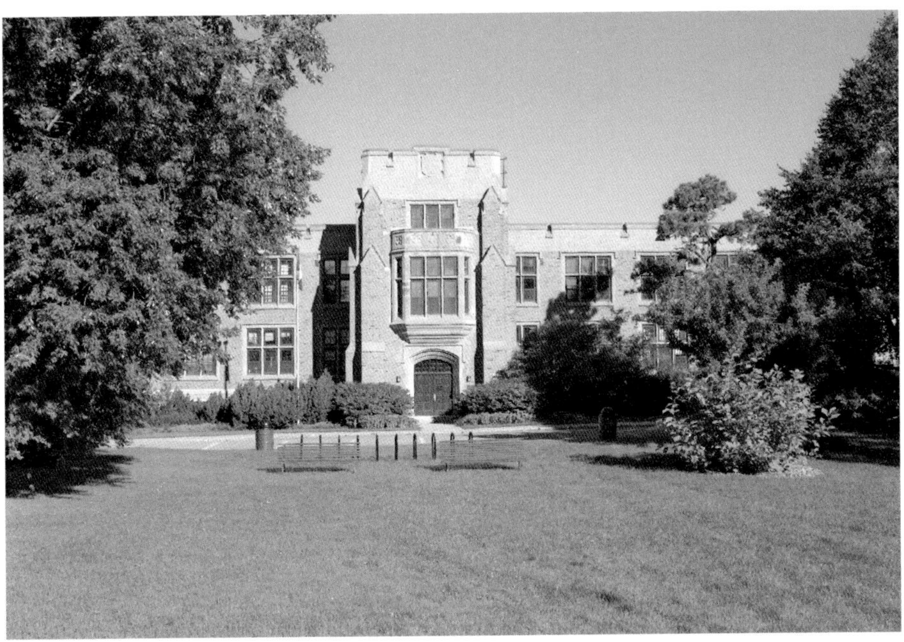

The Saunders Building at the CEF commemorates both father and son.

and feeding of animals and a host of other farm-related topics. On January 30, 1884, a select committee of the House was appointed to "determine the needs for the improvement of Canadian agriculture." Known as the Gigault Committee after its chair, G.A. Gigault, it started by polling farmers about their needs. It sent out 1,500 questionnaires and received 385 replies—a good return even by modern standards. The great majority of responses favoured establishing an experimental farm, appointing an entomologist, establishing a central bureau with statistical information and the publication of handbooks, reports and bulletins. The committee recommended the creation of an experimental farm where varieties of foreign grains, trees and fertilizers could be tested for their applicability to Canada. The farm could also distribute samples of seeds and plants throughout Canada.

The committee also consulted some fourteen witnesses and reported to Parliament on March 21, 1884. Its members recommended the creation of a bureau within the Department of Agriculture and experimental farms that could operate in conjunction with the proposed bureau. Parliament appointed Professor William Saunders to "make further and detailed studies on the worth of the experimental farms." Saunders reported to the minister of agriculture in February 1886. In April 1886, Sir John Carling recommend that the House establish such a farm system, with no statements in opposition registered. Nearly half the Canadian population at the time were farmers, so little opposition would have been expected. The supporting bill was a passed on May 11, 1886, and the creation of the Experimental Farm System was established with five farms at the beginning. The Central Experimental Farm was created in Ottawa and remains to the current day.

THE HOTEL SCANDAL OF THE 1870S

Related to the coming of science and the government's purchase of the building at the corner of Sussex and George for the Geological Survey of Canada, there is a bigger story to be told about that building in particular. The building still stands, but the GSC has moved on.

The building dates back to 1838, when it was known as both the British and the Ottawa Hotel. It was so successful that it was enlarged, improved and even redecorated in 1853. Its owner, Donald McArthur, had a passion for geology and maintained a private rock collection that he displayed in public view, thus establishing a link to the geological purpose it was later to serve. The building also served as a military barracks during the Fenian Raids from 1866 to 1870 and then reverted back to its former use as a hotel when the danger had passed.

The first hotel after the threat of raids had subsided opened in 1873 and failed miserably. In 1875, it was reopened as the Clarendon Hotel after refurbishing and remodeling. That hotel failed also, but it was in this era and while in possession of new owners that the scandal occurred, smearing the name of a young parliamentarian from Quebec and making the hotel business even more difficult. The owners of the hotel had an attractive young daughter who claimed that the MP had sexually assaulted her—maybe even on site. The matrons of the town were greatly offended, and the MP was charged under the criminal code of the time. His counterclaim was that he had not assaulted the young lady, and he implied that her parents were trying to extort money to help their already ailing hotel survive financial ruin. After a lengthy trial, with claims and counterclaims, the young MP was exonerated, and no subsequent civil suit followed. The young MP had been vindicated by the courts, but this scandal had cast a shadow on the hotel and on any hope of reviving the business and returning it to its grander days.

The building in question then failed again in 1876 and remained vacant until the government decided to purchase it for the headquarters of the Geological Survey of Canada in 1879. First, it was used as the site of the first exhibition of the Canadian Academy of Fine Arts in 1880, and then it was remodelled for the GSC, which finally took possession in 1881. Interestingly enough, the tribulations of the building and its owners had not yet ended. The GSC had encompassed or at least taken control of a rock collection while in Montreal at McGill University. The problem was that the rock collection had partially belonged to Sir William Logan. The first director of the GSC threatened to sue the government for removing the collection from McGill, as Logan's will had bequeathed his collection to the university. The trustees of the will were famous men in their own right: philosopher George Grant and Sir William Dawson, president of McGill. The threat appears in the public documents, but there is no record of a settlement. We can presume that the matter was settled out of court, as the rock collection has remained with the Geological Survey of Canada. Suffice it to say, this building has seen its share of trouble, and one has to wonder, as it still stands today, if it has any more stories to tell.

The Birth of the National Research Council

Canada is proud to possess one of the best agencies in the world for conducting and coordinating scientific and industrial research: the National Research Council (NRC).

In 1842, the first federal government research agency, the Geological Survey of Canada (GSC), was established in conjunction with McGill University in Montreal. It was followed by the Research Branch of the Department of Agriculture and the forerunners of the Fisheries Research Board of Canada and the Dominion Astronomical Observatory. Little was done in the realm of industrial research or in sectors not related to resource industries. In fact, it was 1963 before a federal department of industry was created with the purpose of enhancing industrial research.

Even the universities did not possess laboratory facilities until the late nineteenth century, as noted by H.M. Tory when he discussed his early scientific education at one of Canada's preeminent universities. The universities were always seeking funding from the various governments but did not appreciate suggestions of how such funding should be spent. During most of the nineteenth century, funding that was secured did not find its way to scientific endeavours. The classics predominated at the time. It really took an international conflict and the advancement of military technology to raise questions about Canada's efforts. The lack of Canadian research capacity was keenly felt at the beginning of World War I in 1914.

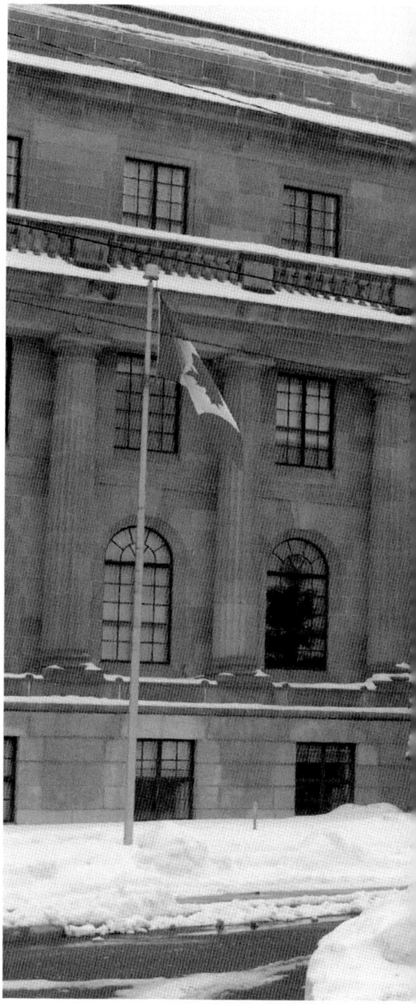

Headquarters of the National Research Council, built in 1933.

On May 25, 1915, twelve people met in the office of Sir George Foster, minister of trade and commerce in the Borden government. Foster was reasonably well read in research problems and needs, having been a member of the Gigault Committee as well as Industrial, which recommended the creation of the Experimental Farm System in 1885. Foster had been reviewing many representations on the necessity to create some sort of institution or agency to coordinate and perhaps even catalyse industrial research. Pressure had intensified since the war had begun the previous August.

Among the twelve attendees were industrial representatives, university scientists and the president of the Royal Canadian Institute. Foster was

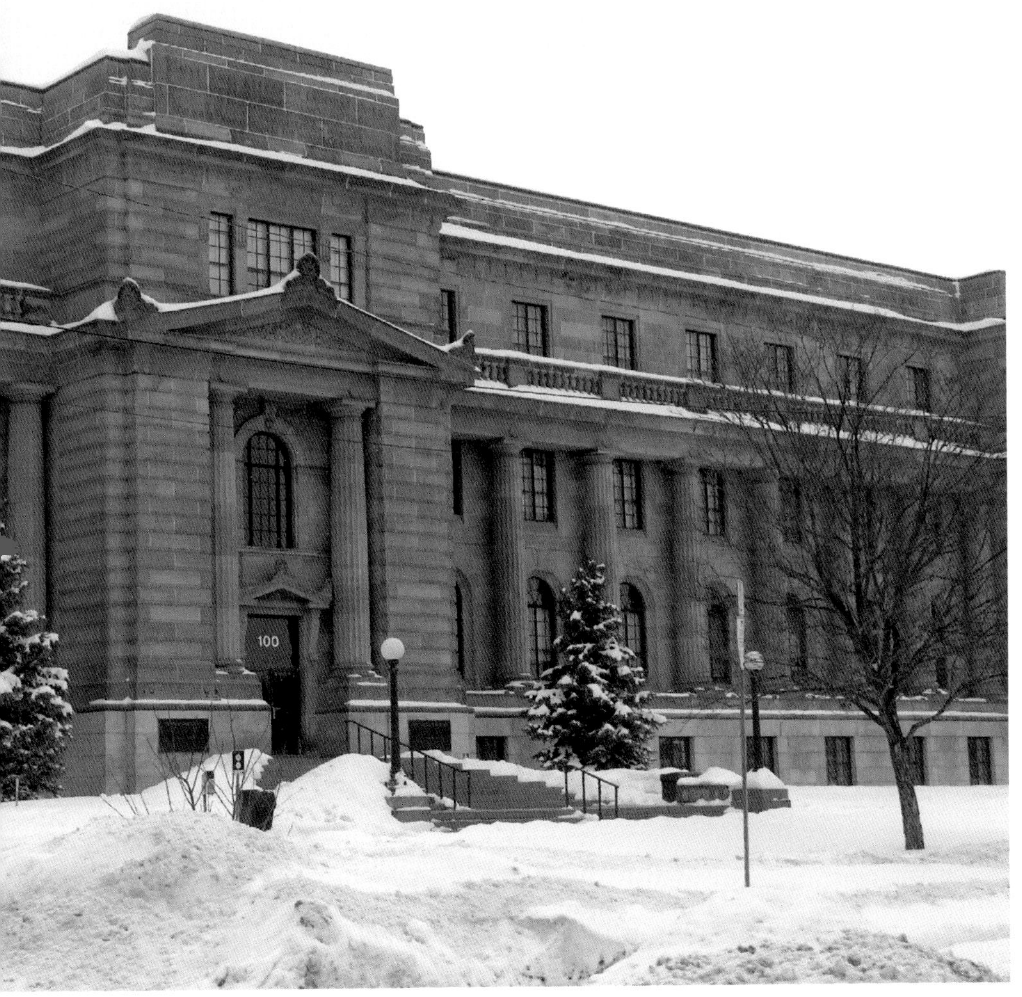

hesitant to organize the meeting as he knew of the pressure to provide university funding that he feared might only provide usable research results to Canadian industry. His feelings were shared by the prime minister, who warned him of the desires of the university scientists. Foster and Borden felt that some sort of an institution was possible but that the scientists might "run riot" if they knew that any money was available. Mel Thistle, who wrote a history of the early development of the NRC, commented on the problems faced, especially the propensity of strong-minded scientists who felt that money should be granted free of administrative controls, which they felt would hamper their ability to operate. Notwithstanding these concerns, a National Advisory Council on Industrial Research (NACSIR) was created to advise the government on the kind of research needed to help the manufacturing industry and the progress of scientific research in general. NACSIR was given an appropriation and the freedom to expend it.

The difficulties implicit in having an organization managed by a group of intelligent, opinionated persons with many conflicting loyalties emerged as early as the first few months of 1917. One of the council's first responsibilities was to compile an inventory of research projects in Canada. In May 1919, Dr. A.B. Macallum, first chair of the NACSIR, expressed his disappointment with the results of the survey. Only thirty-seven of some eight thousand industrial establishments surveyed reported any current research projects, and the bulk of the thirty-seven employed only one person.

The government established a committee of enquiry into scientific and industrial research in Canada, named after H. Cronyn, its chair. It came to the conclusion that some sort of research establishment should be created, a conclusion also adopted by NACSIR in 1916 but not adopted by the government. A review of the testimony before the Cronyn committee, as well as that committee's final recommendation that an institute be established, is very revealing regarding how perceptions of the value of science and technology were changing in Canada. Fourteen witnesses were interviewed, with Dr. Macallum being the first. His opinions were strong, as he believed that scientists must be as free as possible from political and administrative controls. This insistence was to be the cause of many future problems that are still not totally resolved.

While the Cronyn Enquiry results were accepted, difficulty persisted. Politicians felt that the results of research should be immediately useful in industry, while scientists stressed job creation and the need for pure science whose usefulness might be more long term. It took until 1933 before a new National Research Council got its own building and laboratories. Another difficulty was that the universities were of the opinion that the government should increase funding and leave them to spend it as they wished.

Aside from the hesitancy of the government to spend funds, the new organization had to face suspicions from other departments, a lack of trained technologists, political instability and the lack of laboratories. There was no quick and easy way to put science and industry together. Industry wanted useful results, but scientists had more patient, longer-term views. This delayed the creation of laboratories until 1933, just in time to make a useful contribution to World War II, despite the fact that the need was repeated several times by the Cronyn committee and its successors.

THE EARLY DAYS OF THE CIVIL SERVICE: NEPOTISM AND ROBERT BELL

After Confederation in 1867, the federal government was centred in Ottawa. Shortly thereafter, issues arose concerning the representation of not only the number of civil servants of Canadian origin but also the number of civil servants representing the original partners in Confederation.

Michael J. Piva attempted an analysis of the 1871 situation in the book *Ottawa: Making a Capital*, edited by Jeff Keshen and Nicole St. Onge and published in 2001. The analysis is pertinent to Ottawa as it deals with the distribution of civil servants in Ottawa itself and not those in the "outside" service in other parts of the country. There were not many Ottawa civil servants in 1871. Lumber mills employed 1,800 men, compared to about 600 in the "inside" service. What Piva tried to uncover is whether the distribution of origin and salaries earned was equitable in modern terms.

From his analysis, it appears that they were not, but commonly held opinions were questionable. For example, he compared civil servants born in England, Quebec and Ontario, and their distribution was not proportionate. England and Quebec were more highly represented than the Canadians who were born in Ontario. In 1871, appointments were patronage-based rather than based on merit.

It might prove illustrative to review a well-documented case that clearly outlines the concerns of one senior individual regarding the kinds of abuses possible. The arguments made by the person were never made public and never proven but simply are indicative of what

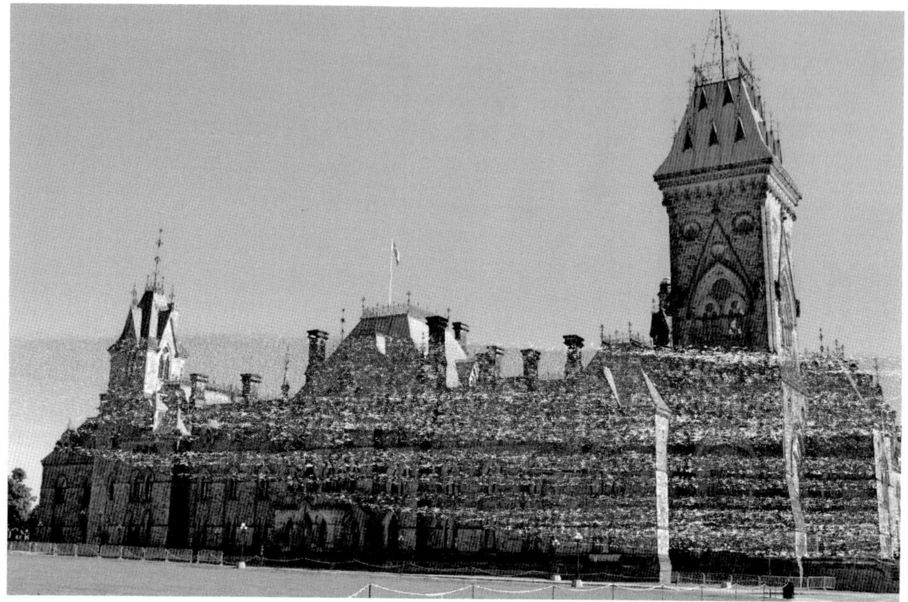

The east block on Parliament hill—the early home of the Civil Service.

possibly happened. The individual was Robert Bell, a senior official of the Geological Survey of Canada, complaining of abuse in a long thirteen-page letter to Sir Clifford Sifton, the minister of the interior in the Laurier government.

Bell was frustrated at the appointment of George Dawson as director of the survey over his head. He argued that he should have been appointed because of his seniority and his legal support of the Liberal Party (whereas the victor had supported the Conservative Party). Bell also accused William Dawson, the president of McGill University, of using his position to have his son, George, advanced ahead of Bell, even though Bell had a better academic record and more experience. This was a common practice before 1918 and was quite possibly true.

In essence, Bell criticized Alfred R.C. Selwyn for his management style and his treatment of employees. Per Bell, Selwyn played favourites, gave preference to certain employees (probably Dawson) in terms of publishing their work, favoured research over practical work and was stingy with the budget. Also, he did not have the support of the mining industry. Bell claimed that Selwyn caused an order-in-council to be passed that gave preference to George Dawson to be acting director when Selwyn was absent. Bell claimed that he had been subject to twenty years of petty persecution. To be fair to Bell, he was not averse to giving credit where he thought it was due. He singled out his old colleague Elkanah Billingsour, former paleontologist and the "finest" naturalist Canada has ever produced. Bell was almost vitriolic in his criticism of those he didn't like and seems to have had a persecution complex.

In conclusion, without discussing the merits of Bell's case, the details of the case and the arguments presented by Piva, nepotism and favouritism likely had a great part to play in early appointments—note that few women were appointed and certainly not to management ranks. It would not be until almost a century after 1871 before that oversight even began to be rectified. The Civil Service was not large, and many people knew one another well. This aided nepotism and favouritism for no other reason than to avoid the time, expense and frustration of hiring outside the inner circle. Better a wolf you know than one you don't know.

Ottawa's Early Military

We remember the sacrifices of the world wars. We also had military units in Ottawa getting ready to go to the Fenian Raids, the Northwest Rebellion and the Boer War. Regardless of the justice or injustice of these events, we still had men willing to risk their lives for the rest of their country. Let's look at our involvement in these conflicts.

Some years ago, Colonel Strome Galloway, who commanded the Royal Canadian Regiment in the battle for Ortona in World War II, summarized the early history of the Ottawa military for the Historical Society of Ottawa, and I am indebted to him for the information found in this chapter. Much of the early history of the military in Ottawa concerns militia or reserve units that were made up of ordinary citizens who "answered the call" when danger threatened. According to Galloway, no regular army fighting unit has ever been garrisoned in Ottawa. This is not true of the RCAF, which based interceptor and reconnaissance squadrons here during the height of the Cold War. However, we are looking at a much earlier period in this chapter.

Interesting events that involved Ottawa citizen soldiers included the Fenian Raids of 1866 and 1870, when the "Civil Service Rifles" were called up to repel invasion if it was necessary. The Governor-General's Foot Guards provided several officers to command the 150 "Voyageurs" who

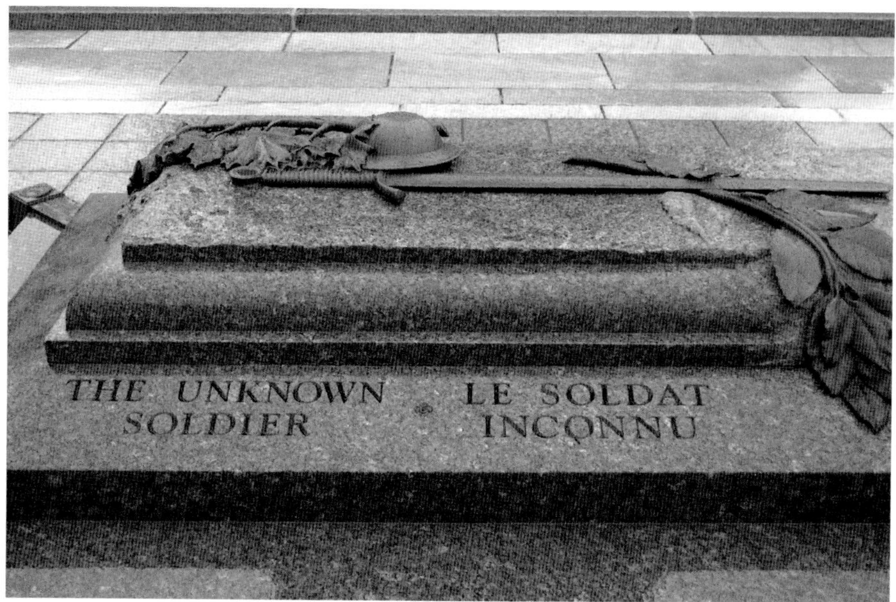

The tomb of the unknown soldier, honouring Canada's war dead.

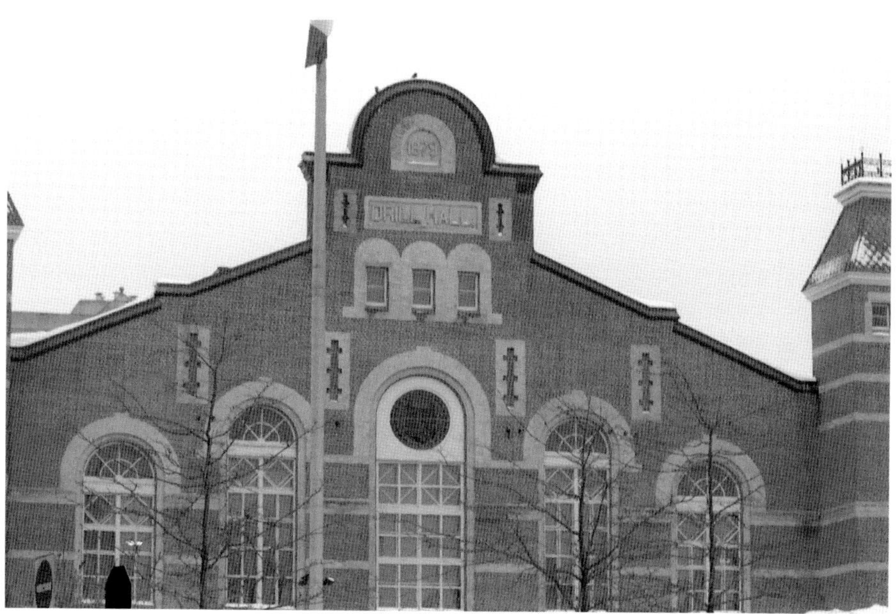

Military drill hall built in 1878. It is still in use.

ferried British troops up the Nile River in 1884. Ottawa provided a group of 50 sharpshooters, mostly from the foot guards, to the troops dispatched to Saskatchewan at the time of the Northwest difficulties in 1885. About 100 men were provided by the 43rd Rifles and the Governor-General's Foot Guards as reinforcements for the Royal Canadian Regiment in the Boer War of 1899. A member of the Rifles was awarded a Queen's Scarf of Honour for his involvement. Queen Victoria personally knitted seven scarfs for special acts of valor in the field. She knitted three for the British forces and one each for Canadian, Australian, New Zealand and South African forces. By the time World War I began, around August 1914, Ottawa troops were fully involved.

The first military unit organized in Ottawa was the Ottawa Volunteer Field Battery, also called the "Bytown Gunners," which still exists today. It was formed in 1855, and its members have served in many conflicts. Its second battery, serving in the Boer War, had among its members John McRae, who was famous for his poem "In Flanders Fields." The Bytown Gunners unit has served in all wars and is particularly famous for the salutes the soldiers fire on Parliament Hill on national occasions, such as Remembrance Day.

The senior infantry regiment in Ottawa is the Governor-General's Foot Guards, formed in 1861 in Quebec City as the Civil Service Rifles. When government moved to Ottawa, so did the Rifles. During the Fenian Raids, all male civil servants were conscripted to guard government buildings—our first example of military conscription. In 1872, it was considered that the new Dominion should have a regiment of guards similar to those who guarded the queen in London. The unit was modelled on the Coldstream Guards of the British army. Colours were first presented to the guards by the wife of the governor-general in 1874, and the Cartier Square Armory was constructed to house them and others in 1878. By royal decree, this regiment has military precedence over all other Canadian regiments.

In 1881, the 43rd Ottawa and Carleton Rifles became the Duke of Cornwall's Own Rifles, and in 1933, its name was changed to the Cameron Highlanders of Ottawa. In 1872, an Ottawa troop of cavalry was organized that became the forerunner of the 4th Princess Louis Dragoon Guards and the 4th Hussars. We stopped using horses for war after World War I, so most horse regiments became armoured units, using tanks instead.

Other units assembled in Ottawa but were not really Ottawa units. The first was in 1898—the Yukon Field Force, which was mustered to aid the Royal Northwest Mounted Police in policing the Yukon in the face of the lawlessness associated with the Yukon Gold Rush. In December 1899, with the Royal Canadian regiment already on the way to South Africa, Lord Strathcona, then Canada's high commissioner in Great Britain, offered a blank cheque to recruit a cavalry regiment to serve in South Africa. This unit became known as the Lord Strathcona's Horse. In 1914, another generous person put up $100,000 of his own money to form a regiment to be named after the then governor-general's daughter, Princess Patricia. This unit became known as the Princess Patricia's Canadian Light Infantry and has just finished a tour of duty in Afghanistan. It also served in both world wars, as did the Lord Strathcona's Horse, on horses in World War I and then in tanks in World War II. Both units assembled in Ottawa. All of the units mentioned have links to Ottawa (and they represent only army units). Ottawa has contributed much to Canada's military history, and that fact should be better known.

Part V
Trials and Tragedies

What the Great Fire of 1870 Brought

It had been a dry year in 1870, and fire was a real hazard. In their book *Carleton Saga*, Harry and Olive Walker told the story of a great fire that almost burned down Ottawa itself. The fire proved a need for a dependable water supply and firefighting equipment, and the city fathers took steps in that direction that were to prove helpful thirty years later in 1900. However, some of the water mains established are still functioning today, as things were built to last then.

There was no identifiable source for the 1870 fire, although lightning was suspected. It could have been started by human error as well. There had been a long drought that summer, and no rain had fallen for two months. On August 18, the fire, moving at five miles per hour, struck the southwestern limits of the city. It quickly started consuming homes, and many fled before it. By 8:00 p.m., the streets were empty, dust and smoke were everywhere and hundreds spent the night in rivers wading and standing in the water to escape the flames and smoke. At the fire front, volunteer bucket brigades drawing water from horse-drawn carts fought the blaze. There were no fire brigades or any city water supplies available. Water came from the Ottawa and Rideau Rivers, and there were only three water pumps fed by carts.

By the morning of the nineteenth, an estimated two thousand citizens were homeless as the fire moved along Richmond Road. Two thousand men were fighting at the fire front along where Bell Street is now located. An emergency fund of $1,000 was created to provide immediate help. At the time, all the men from an estimated population of twenty-one thousand were called out to battle the flames. All businesses were closed, and there was no visibility along the river. The military garrison was also called out; track ties were burning, and a main line of defence was established at Dow's Lake. An emergency dam called "St. Louis Dam" was created to control the spread of fire, and its remains can still be seen at low water. The fire stretched from the middle of the Driveway to the naval station. Flames reached just beyond where the Central Experimental Farm is today.

A house owned by the McGrath family was commandeered for the firefighters and stocked with beer, cheese and crackers; it was also constantly replenished. You couldn't tell the firemen from the free-loaders, according to Harry and Olive Walker. The temporary dam broke, but the spreading water saved the city. Most of the devastation occurred in the west end, especially around present-day Bell's Corners.

It was generally agreed that high winds and a lack of water had made the fire spread more quickly. This fire and the Great Chicago Fire of 1871 seemed to spur politicians into action. Tap water came to Ottawa in 1875 in a system designed by engineer Thomas Keefer. Beforehand, water was taken from the Ottawa River and delivered door to door—so much for modern ideas of sanitation! For the next few years, things went smoothly, until fire struck again in 1900.

THE CITY BURNS: THE GREAT FIRE OF 1900

You would think that the 1870 fire would have taught more lessons than it did, but as with human efforts generally, there is always more to learn.

On April 26, 1900, a defective chimney on the Gatineau side of the Ottawa River started a fire that will be long remembered. Seven people were killed, and fifteen thousand were left homeless; 20 percent of housing in Ottawa and 42 percent in the city of Hull were destroyed. Damage was estimated at $9.5 million in 1900 dollars. The disaster was heard around the world, and $957,000 in aid was received, including a small donation from as far as Chile.

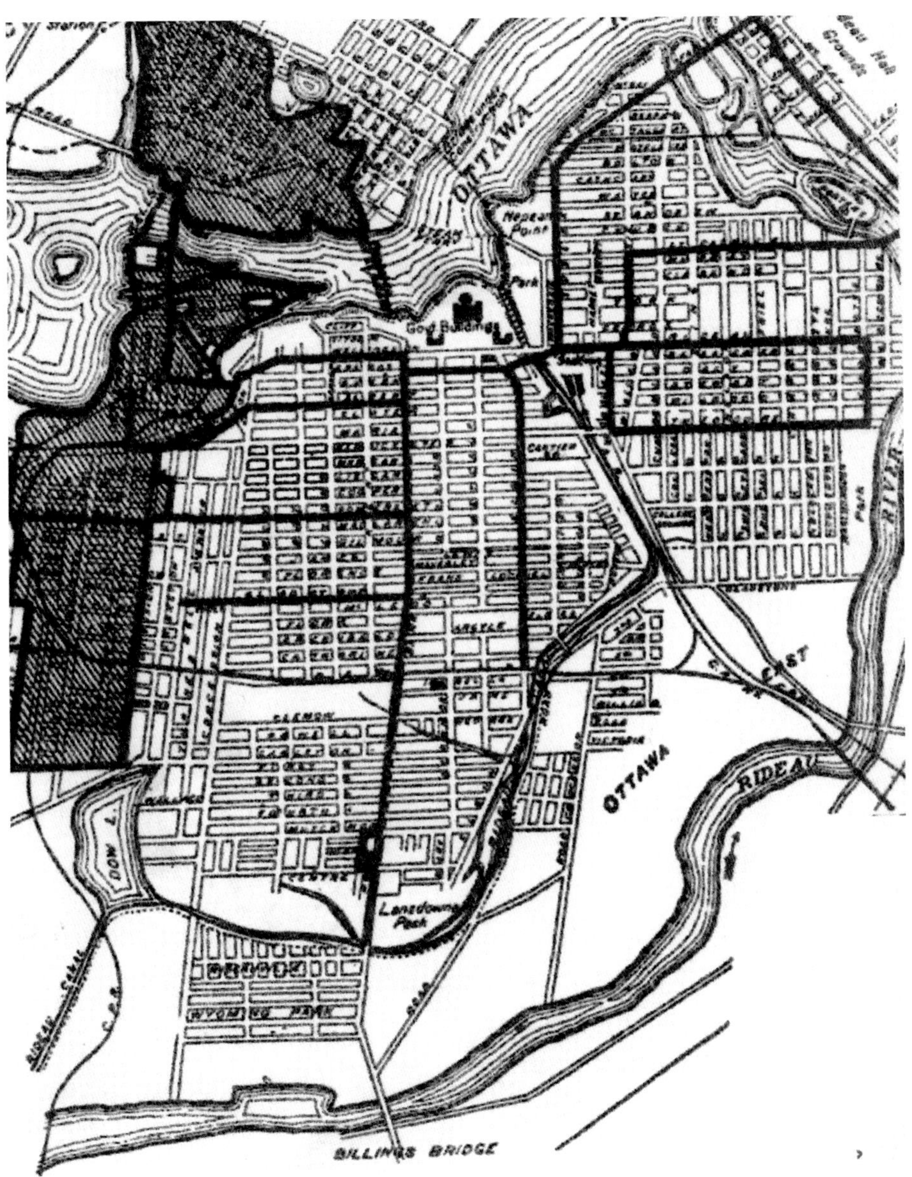

Map of area burned in 1870. *Belden.*

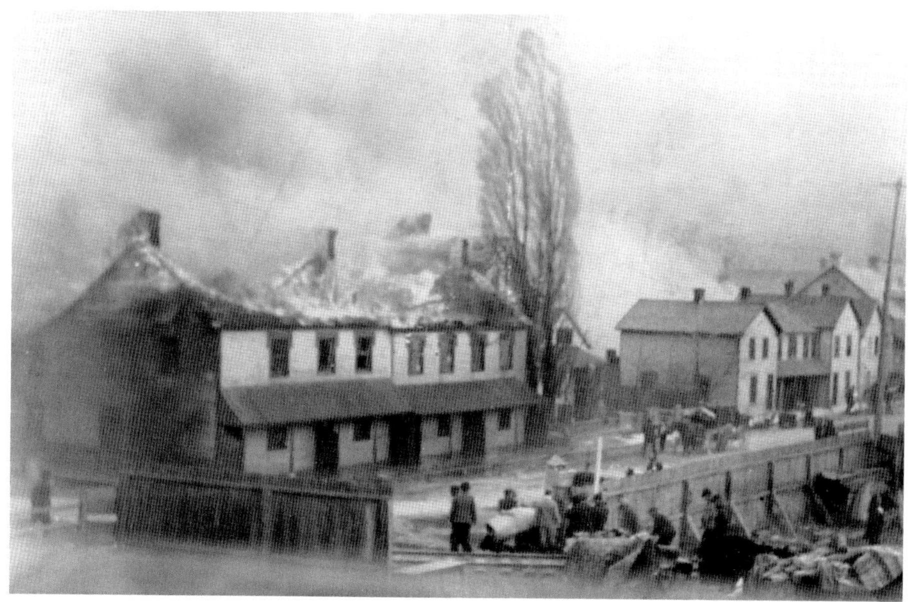

A photo of a house in the fire of 1900. *National Archives of Canada.*

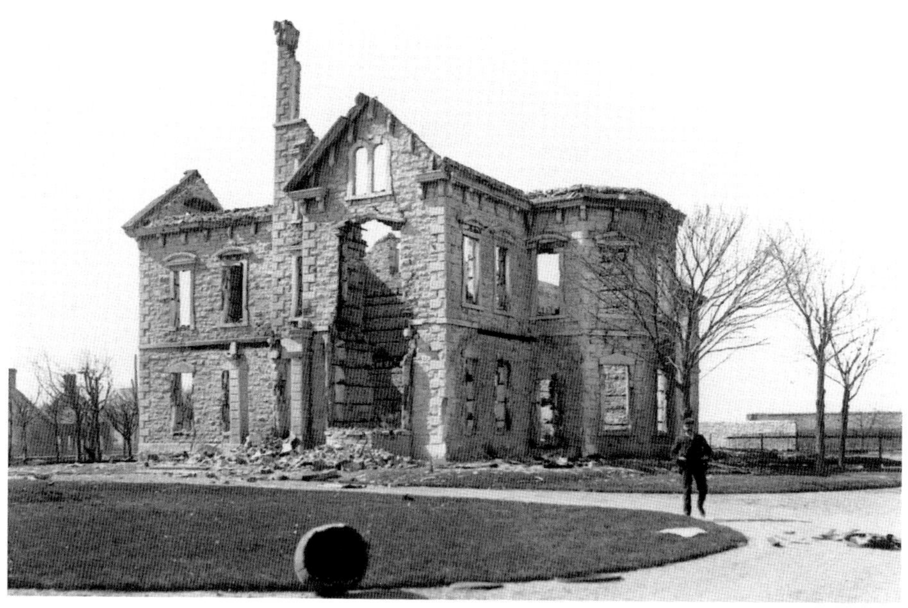

Burned-out house from 1900 fire. *Ottawa City Archives.*

Housing at the time was nearly all wooden, and the fire was easily able to jump from house to house. It didn't help the situation that a number of lumberyards were situated between the two cities, and these only added to the conflagration. The fire attacked the same swath as had the 1870 fire, from Lebreton Flats to Dow's Lake, and again Dow's Lake helped block the path of the fire.

Tent cities sprang up to house the dispossessed. Disease spread rapidly in crowded tents, and more died from disease than from the fire. Aid was requested from Toronto and Montreal and was soon forthcoming. This was badly needed, as the two fire engines—the Conqueror and La France—purchased after the fire thirty years prior were engulfed by the quickly moving flames. A fire engine arrived from Montreal in less than two hours.

Despite all efforts, two-thirds of Hull was damaged, and about 40 percent of available housing was destroyed. Only 23 percent of Hull's losses were covered by insurance, as compared to 50 percent of losses in Ottawa. In percentages of homes destroyed, 14 percent of Ottawa was lost, compared to 42 percent of Hull. The cost of the fire approached $9.5 million in 1900 dollars, and aid totalled $957,000, which was about 10 percent of the losses.

The cost in human life was also severe. Although seven lives were lost directly because of the fire, more died from pneumonia and other diseases contracted as a result of living in tent cities in the wintertime. While no figures are readily available, given the lack of antibiotics and a lower technical standard of medical care, it is certain that the fire indirectly was responsible for a good many more deaths and disabilities.

Lessons learned from both fires were improved on, and no other major fires occurred until the Parliament buildings burned in 1916, a fire limited to a small area but one that had a much larger impact on the national psyche.

PARLIAMENT BUILDINGS BURN

Talk about fires! Not only did major portions of the city burn in 1870 and 1900, but the crown of the city, the Parliament buildings, nearly burned to the ground as well in 1916. What is it with fires and this city?

On February 3, 1916, smoke was detected near the Parliamentary reading room. Within a few hours, the centre block was completely destroyed, except for

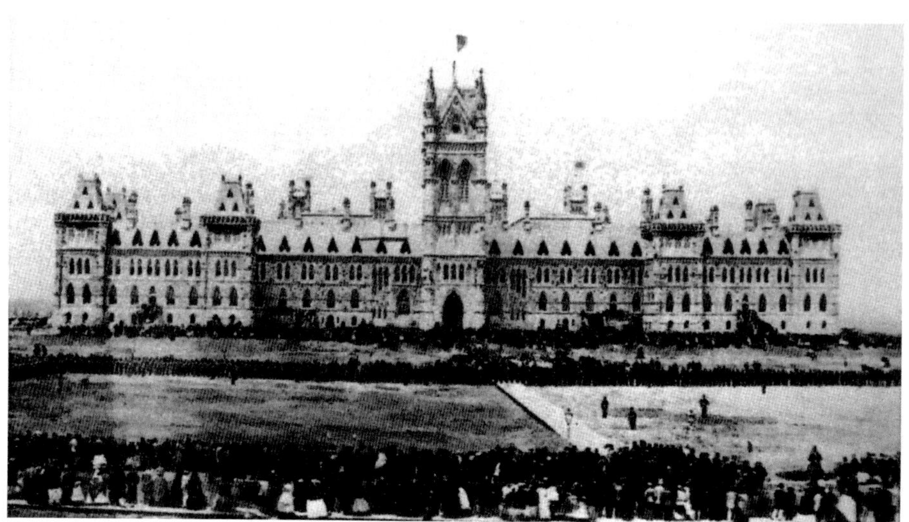

Canadian Parliament buildings before the fire of 1916. *Belden.*

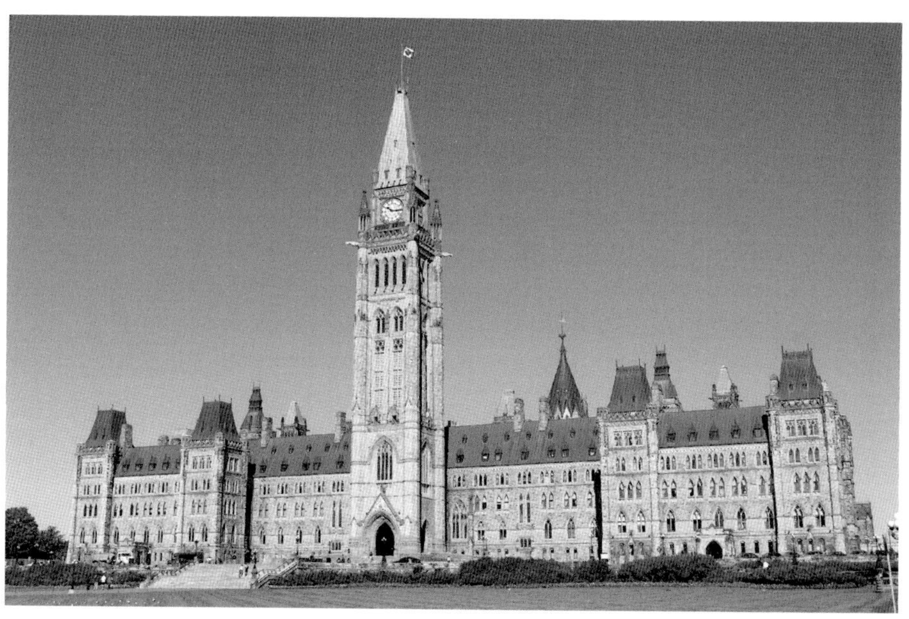

The nation's capital—the centre block of Parliament. *Author's collection.*

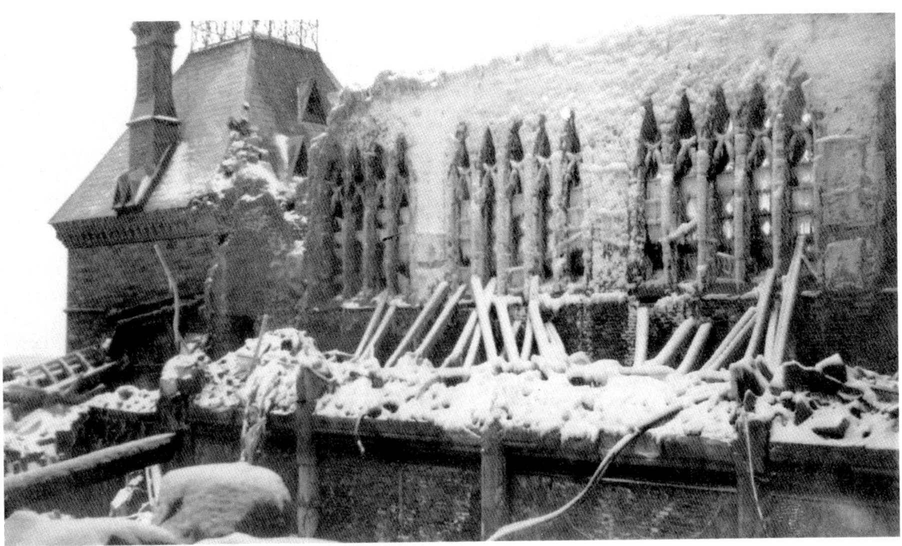

Damage from the 1916 fire at Parliament. *Ottawa City Archives.*

the Parliamentary Library. The investigation that followed found the cause to be accidental. Rumors abounded, though, that it was an enemy action—Canada was at war with Germany at the time. The buildings on Parliament Hill had all been constructed between 1859 and 1866, and a detailed report on the event by G.W. Shorter of the National Research Council described the event in better detail. At the time, Prime Minister Robert Borden (whose face is found on the $100 bill) was the leader of the country. The fire warning interrupted a debate on fish marketing, and people hastily retreated to safety. The fire spread quickly, and the roof of the centre block collapsed at 9:30 p.m. At 1:21 a.m., the bell tower collapsed. By 3:00 a.m. on February 4, the fire was largely under control. There were iron safety doors connecting the centre block with the library, and they were undoubtedly the reason why the library did not burn.

There were seven casualties as a result of this fire. The body of an MP from Yarmouth, Nova Scotia, was discovered near the Commons Reading Room, where smoking is believed to have been one of the possible causes of the fire. The body of Rene Laplante, an accounting clerk for the House of Commons, was discovered two days later. Albert Sevigny was the House Speaker at the time, and two of his guests were found burned in a corridor, as they had returned to the building to get their fur coats. Finally, the bodies of a policeman and two civil servants were found crushed by a wall. All these losses are spelled out in more detail in Shorter's report.

After the fire, Parliament resumed meeting in what is today the Museum of Natural History on Argyle Street. It took four years to rebuild the Parliament buildings. The first time Parliament met in the new building was on February 26, 1920. The centre block was completely finished in 1922, and the Peace Tower was finished in 1927. A funny anecdote goes with this story. The Royal Canadian Mounted Police (RCMP) assigned two officers to guard the Parliamentary Library in 1916, as it was the only portion of the building still intact. Strangely enough, the assignment only changed in the mid-1960s, almost fifty years after the fire. The RCMP certainly took its duty seriously.

Archibald Lampman, a Canadian Poet

It was a typical cold winter day in Ottawa in 1899 when Archibald Lampman died. He was mourned by his friends and family at the time and has since become mourned by many Canadians as a poet who, like Shelley and Keats, died before his time. He lived only thirty-eight years, just sixteen of them in Ottawa, but here he produced much of his best work.

Lampman was well educated and considered to be from a good family, as his father was an Anglican minister. He graduated with honours in classics from Trinity College in Toronto, where he was active on the student newspaper, the *Rouge et Noir.* After a try at being a schoolteacher, he was appointed to the Post Office Department in the Langevin Block in Ottawa in 1885 at the then comfortable salary of $450 per annum. He became a family man, marrying Maude Playter in 1887, and they had two children, Natalie and Archibald. By the time of his death in 1899, Lampman was earning $1,200 per year. This was a very good salary, although he found the work to be tedious and boring.

Lampman was never in good health, as he had contracted rheumatic fever in his youth, and he was delicate, with a particularly weak heart. The Lampmans lost their son in 1894, and Archibald never really recovered from the tragedy, although he kept his mind busy. His friend, another poet, Duncan Campbell Scott, blamed Lampman's continued weakness on the fact that he had always driven himself too hard. Even Lampman himself commented on his personal health in a poem he wrote after a very physical trip he took with Scott:

Are you broken with the din of the street?
Are you sickened of your thin hands and feet?
Are you bowed and bended double?
With a weight of care and trouble,
Are you spectral, with a skin like a sheet?

Lampman wrote most of his work at the post office, where he found that his job did not demand all of his time, and he continually commented on the routine nature of his job. He was, of course, more interested in the recognition of his poetical work. He had been elected to the Royal Society of Canada by his peers, but his poetry was not popular with the people. Only an elite few who were his friends and colleagues in the academic circles he frequented took any interest.

Whatever the company he kept, he was mourned by many, and he is now regarded as one of Canada's finest poets of the nineteenth century. He died on February 5, 1899, and there is no finer way to remember him than to quote the sonnet he wrote only a few days after his son's death in 1894. It is reproduced here from the Beechwood Cemetery, where he and his son are interred:

Here the dead sleep—the quiet dead. No sound
Disturbs them ever, and no storm dismays.
Winter mid snow caresses the tired ground,
And the wind roars about the woodland ways.
Springtime and summer and red autumn pass,
With leaf and bloom and pipe of wind and bird,
And old earth puts forth her tender grass,
By them unfelt, unheeded and unheard.
Our centuries to them are but strokes
In the dim gamut of some far-off chime.
Unaltering rest their perfect being cloaks—
A thing too vast to hear or feel or see—
Children of Silence and Eternity,
They know no season but the end of time.

The Assassination of Thomas D'Arcy McGee and the Fenian Impact on Confederation

Back in April 1868, the only assassination of a federal MP happened right here on Sparks Street. He was, in fact, a "Father of Confederation," a man who had played an active part in the constitutional conference at Charlottetown, Prince Edward Island, in 1864 that brought us the British North America Act of 1867. Charlottetown was the original conference concerned with the foundation of Canada as a nation. The murdered man's name was Thomas D'Arcy McGee, and he was of Irish extraction. The man who was convicted of murdering him, Patrick Whelan, the last individual subject to a public hanging in Canada, was also an Irishman and was rumoured to be a member of the Fenian Brotherhood.

The members of the Fenian Brotherhood were dedicated to freeing Ireland from British rule and were the last official invaders of Canada in 1866 and again in 1870. The presence of the Fenians, who were largely U.S. Civil War veterans, probably added extra pressure to the idea of forming the Canadian nation. Their aim was to conquer Canada and then trade it back to Britain for Irish freedom. McGee had begun his political career as a strong proponent of Irish freedom, but he became a stronger proponent of Canadian Confederation and argued against Fenian ambitions; this might have convinced the Fenians that he was a traitor to their cause. In any event, McGee was shot in the back of the head outside his lodgings at 142 Sparks Street on April 7, 1868. He was returning late from the House of Commons, and there were no witnesses to his shooting.

McGee was born in Ireland in 1825 and first came to Canada in 1857 after a career as a journalist and political activist both in Ireland and the United States. He argued vigorously for Irish freedom but was opposed to the measures expressed by the Fenian Brotherhood. He rose in Canadian politics and, at the time of the Charlottetown conference, was a minister of agriculture in John A. MacDonald's government. He was a fiery orator in the days when oratory was an art form. There are several pictures of McGee in Charlotte Gray's excellent book *The Museum Called Canada*. There is also a pamphlet available from the Bytown Museum that fully discusses McGee's career.

Needless to say, McGee's death caused an uproar in local circles. Extreme pressure was exerted on the local police authorities to find, arrest and punish the perpetrator. Suspicion fell on a local Fenian, Patrick Whelan, and Gray's book has examples of the wanted posters offering substantial rewards for Whelan's capture, even though there was little evidence available to connect him to the crime. He was eventually captured and incarcerated in the Ottawa gaol. The story of Whelan's trial, conviction and execution is a story in itself and appears later in this book.

McGee's funeral in Montreal was a large one, with literally thousands of people lining the streets. Special testimonial dinners were held in both Ottawa and Montreal, and speeches were made. The threat of the Fenians was underscored. In those days, it was typical to make a plaster cast of a famous dead person's face so that people could remember what the deceased looked like. This was especially true if no painting existed. While early photography was still rapidly developing, it was not yet to the level of popularity it would later enjoy. One problem existed: McGee had been shot in the back of the head, so there was probably extreme facial damage. Therefore, to commemorate McGee's oratorical skills, a plaster cast was made of his hand, with which he often used to gesticulate while making his speeches. A picture of this cast appears in Gray's book, but you only have to visit the Bytown Museum to see the real thing. As mentioned before, the museum has a section devoted to the memory of McGee, and the death cast is there together with other mementos. For a while, the museum also exhibited the gun that was used to shoot McGee. This gun belonged to a descendant of the judge who tried Whelan, but it was recently acquired by a national museum, which loaned it to the Bytown for the exhibit.

The next time you have occasion to walk down the Sparks Street mall, between Metcalfe and O'Connor, look for the plaque that marks the spot where Thomas D'Arcy McGee was shot. Who says Ottawa doesn't have interesting stories to tell?

The Fenians and Confederation, 1866–1870

In the years between the end of the U.S. Civil War and the Confederation of Canada on July 1, 1867, and even afterwards, an external military threat was of concern to Canada and undoubtedly had an effect on the drive for Confederation.

The Fenians were principally based in New York City, where they wore grandiose uniforms and spoke of freeing Ireland from British domination.

They gathered funds from Irish expatriates; even shop girls contributed a few pennies each week. The Fenians planned to attack Canada from several different directions but really didn't succeed at any of them; they had moderate success in the fight at Ridgway in southern Ontario. Other attacks took place in the Maritimes at Campobello Island, up the old attack route along Lake Champlain and even in the West.

The first attack at Campobello Island was alarming but became a complete fiasco, so much so that authorities thought that the Fenian movement was "full of sound and fury, signifying nothing." But the attack had been anticipated and measures taken, and its failure made it seem reasonable that the Fenians could not mount a serious attack. This attitude changed quickly as events took place near Buffalo and across the border near Fort Erie, Ontario. A battle ensued (at Ridgeway) in June 1866 that served to alarm MacDonald in Ottawa and give a last push in favour of Confederation to Nova Scotia and New Brunswick. Organized and experienced veterans of the Civil War in the United States were matched against hastily summoned militia. Fenian reports noted that the Canadian troops at Ridgeway were all Canadian militia volunteers.

The hopes of the Fenians that Irish members of the Canadian militia would support them were soon dashed. On June 2, 1866, on a limestone ridge near the village of Ridgeway and close to Fort Erie, Ontario, a force of irregular Fenians defeated the local militia, composed of some 850 men, including the Queen's Own Rifles, who were at least partially trained. The Canadians seemed to prevail until confusion was introduced by a variety of factors, and the Canadians withdrew, leaving the Fenians in possession of the field after a bayonet charge broke the inexperienced Canadians. The Fenians numbered about 800 at the battle. Casualties were light—only 15 from both sides. Expecting that reinforcements would join the militia, including British troops, the Fenians withdrew to Fort Erie, fought another short battle and then returned to the United States, where between 800 and 1,000 surrendered to U.S. authorities.

The press, as so often happens, exaggerated the significance of the battle, arguing that the results showed that local militia troops could not adequately defend Canada. This must have encouraged the idea of Confederation because on July 1, 1867, the first four provinces joined to form the Dominion of Canada.

A Fenian Punished: The Trial and Execution of Patrick Whelan

On February 11, 1869, in the Carleton County gaol, Patrick James Whelan was hanged for the murder of Thomas D'Arcy McGee. He went to the gallows protesting his innocence, and without all of the modern forensic evidence we are so accustomed to employing, there is no way we can ever be sure that he was truly guilty. There are some who believe that he was innocent and that his conviction was rushed to show the efficiency of the police, prosecutors and the government of the day.

The murder of McGee had taken place the previous April, and Whelan was arrested within twenty hours. The basis of his conviction was his possession of a revolver of the same calibre as the murder weapon, stories that he was a Fenian and the testimony of a person who had shared his cell in the gaol who swore that Whelan had confessed to him. This evidence was enough to convict Whelan and led to the last public hanging in Canada, right here in Ottawa. Five thousand people attended the event. Whelan was buried on the grounds of the gaol, but no one knows exactly where. Remains were discovered some years later, but they could not be confirmed as those of Whelan. Whelan's ghost is said to haunt the gaol, still protesting his innocence. Public hangings were banned in Canada about five months after the execution.

Whelan was of Irish extraction, having been born in County Galway circa 1840. He was a tailor by occupation and apparently was considered good at it. He came to Ottawa from Montreal in 1867 and was employed by the firm of Peter Eagleson. The Canadian Online Encyclopedia describes him as "skilled at his trade, fond of horses, shooting, dancing and drink." This would describe my own Irish ancestors and many current Irish Canadians! While he was an apprentice tailor in Quebec City after 1865, he volunteered for military duty to oppose Fenian invasions of Canada. He married Bridget Boyle in 1867 and made his home in Ottawa. Perhaps a dedicated researcher can find where his residence in Ottawa was or perhaps his immigration record. Ship landing records are on file at the National Library and Archives from 1865 forward. Names and residences are in the city directories.

To the Canada of 1866–67, the Fenians were a scary presence. Mostly Irish expatriates, and many of them hardened veterans of the U.S. Civil War (both Union and Confederate), they were dedicated to conquering Canada to hold as ransom for Ireland's freedom from Britain. They invaded Canada in 1866 and defeated a hastily organized force of militia and some British regulars at Lime Ridge near Fort Erie. They hoped for an Irish uprising in

Canada, and when that did not occur, they retreated to the United States, where they continued to agitate. Another attempt was made south of Montreal in 1870. All the details can be found in Hereward Senior's book *The Last Invasion of Canada* for those interested.

Whelan was said to be sympathetic to this group, but there is little if any hard evidence to go on. Why did he volunteer to fight the Fenians in 1866? There are several facts that suggest that he might have been a scapegoat. There was intense political interest in his trial, as evidenced by the fact that the prime minister, Sir John A. MacDonald, sat beside the presiding judge during the initial trial. The judge was William Richards, who was appointed to the Court of Queen's Bench after the trial just in time to preside over the appeal. The vote to reject the appeal was two to one, with Richards casting the deciding vote. While historians are not supposed to use today's standards to make judgments on past events, there seems to be grounds for suspicion at the very least.

A play, *Blood on the Moon*, was written that queries the conviction, and the song "The Hangman's Eyes" was composed about Whelan's execution. A little-known historical fact is that the real Fenians who invaded Canada were originally sentenced to death, but then the sentence was commuted to life in prison. All of the individuals concerned were released from prison within a decade of the events, except for one individual who died of natural causes during his incarceration. A review of government records indicates that a question of what correspondence there had been about these prisoners was not answered in the House on the recommendation of a House review committee. If this kind of generous treatment was afforded to the real Fenians, then why not Whelan? An answer to that question eludes us to this day.

Being Poor in Ottawa

While the surviving calendars, photographs and newspaper reports from a century ago make Ottawa out to be a kind of winter wonderland, little has been said about those less fortunate and the struggles they faced during the bitter winter weather. A recent report written by James McRostee for the Historical Society of Ottawa paints a rather grim picture, drawn from the winter of 1891.

The principal employment in the city was found in different aspects of the timber industry, which happened to be in the major slumps in general during the 1890s. It must also be remembered that a very limited safety net existed and was principally directed by churches. The churches would primarily give help to those such as widows, orphans and those physically unable to work due to a handicap such as blindness. The work ethic that predominated was that individuals were responsible for themselves, and if they were not able to take care of themselves, it was because they must have been lazy.

Winters are cold in Ottawa, and fuel at the time consisted of wood or coal. The prices were raised when winter demand was high. Wages were reduced, and there was no welfare system in place at the time. Foodstuffs and supply prices were increased as the supply diminished over time. The winter in 1891–92 was particularly tough, and many were out of work.

McRostee's report gives us some statistics to mull over. First, in 1890, the local newspaper published an estimate of the amount of income necessary to support a family, including food, shelter and education. The figure was $1.50 per day for a six-day work week, totalling $9.00 per week. The following indicates the average wages earned in 1891: a sawmill hand, $7.00 to $9.50 per week; a lumber mill yardman, $7.39 weekly; and casual labourers, $1.00 to $1.25 per day (when the work could be found). Historian E. McKenna estimated that the average single man in Ottawa made $9.80 for a fifty-eight-hour workweek, while women and children made less. Workweeks averaged fifty-eight to sixty hours, or an eleven-and-a-half-hour day, with a full half day on Saturday included. Only the general labourers for the City of Ottawa were fortunate enough to have nine-hour days.

However, even with historian E. McKenna's estimate, it can readily be seen that few of the named workers earned the $9.00 per week that was considered necessary, let alone the $9.80 calculated by McKenna. His sample might have contained some higher-paid workers. Additionally, no allowances were made for the problems of winter unemployment and winter price increases, especially for fuel in an abnormally cold winter. Coupled with poor wages, Ottawa workers faced the problem of unsanitary housing conditions. To quote a report on Dalhousie Ward in 1893 by the city sanitation inspector, "A large number of houses now occupied are entirely unfit for habitation." He went on to describe three houses as "so foul I would strongly recommend that the occupants be notified to leave." Those poor standards of living affected health in the days when there was no sick leave and when anyone unable to work was simply not paid. Influenza doubled the sickness and death rate in January and February 1890, and the winter of 1891 was even worse.

In summary, the working poor could not make enough for a living existence, layoffs exacerbated the problem and illness was everywhere. Diseases such as typhoid fever, diphtheria and bronchitis raised the death rate in the months between December and April. Children as young as twelve were working twelve-hour days in J.R. Booth's sawmill as a family coping mechanism.

Coupled with these economic conditions was the social attitude that the poor were responsible for their own situation, and many were ashamed of being poor. The prevalent idea among all classes was that poverty could be attributed to a failure of character rather than economic or environmental reasons. "Workers should be more thrifty," it was said.

Under these circumstances, it would be reasonable to assume that labour unions would have had little problem organizing workers, but this was actually not so. It would take more progressive attitudes and an expanding economy before those problems could be tackled.

Part VI
Things Are a'Changing

Boats on the Rideau Canal in the Nation's Capital

Except for professional historians, few are aware that the beginning of the steamboat era was at the same time as the construction of the Rideau Canal. In fact, the first steamboat on the Great Lakes (1817) predated the completion of the canal by some fifteen years. The planners of the Rideau saw the canal as a moneymaking transportation route as well as the military highway for which it was intended. In fact, Colonel By estimated an annual flow of eight thousand passengers up and down the canal. In 2007, the Historical Society of Ottawa published a pamphlet by Mike Nelles celebrating the naming of the canal as a World Heritage Site. Nelles's article paints a detailed picture of the operation of steamboats on the canal, and readers may wish to consult it and the endnotes, which give an excellent overview of the original sources on the subject. All I can do in this chapter is present a summation of the subject in the hopes of creating an interest in the topic. Nelles pointed out that, by the time the canal was completed, "steamboats were fast becoming the principal method of transport on the lakes and rivers of Upper Canada."

The Rideau Waterway remained an important route for business and commerce until it was rendered obsolete by transportation developments

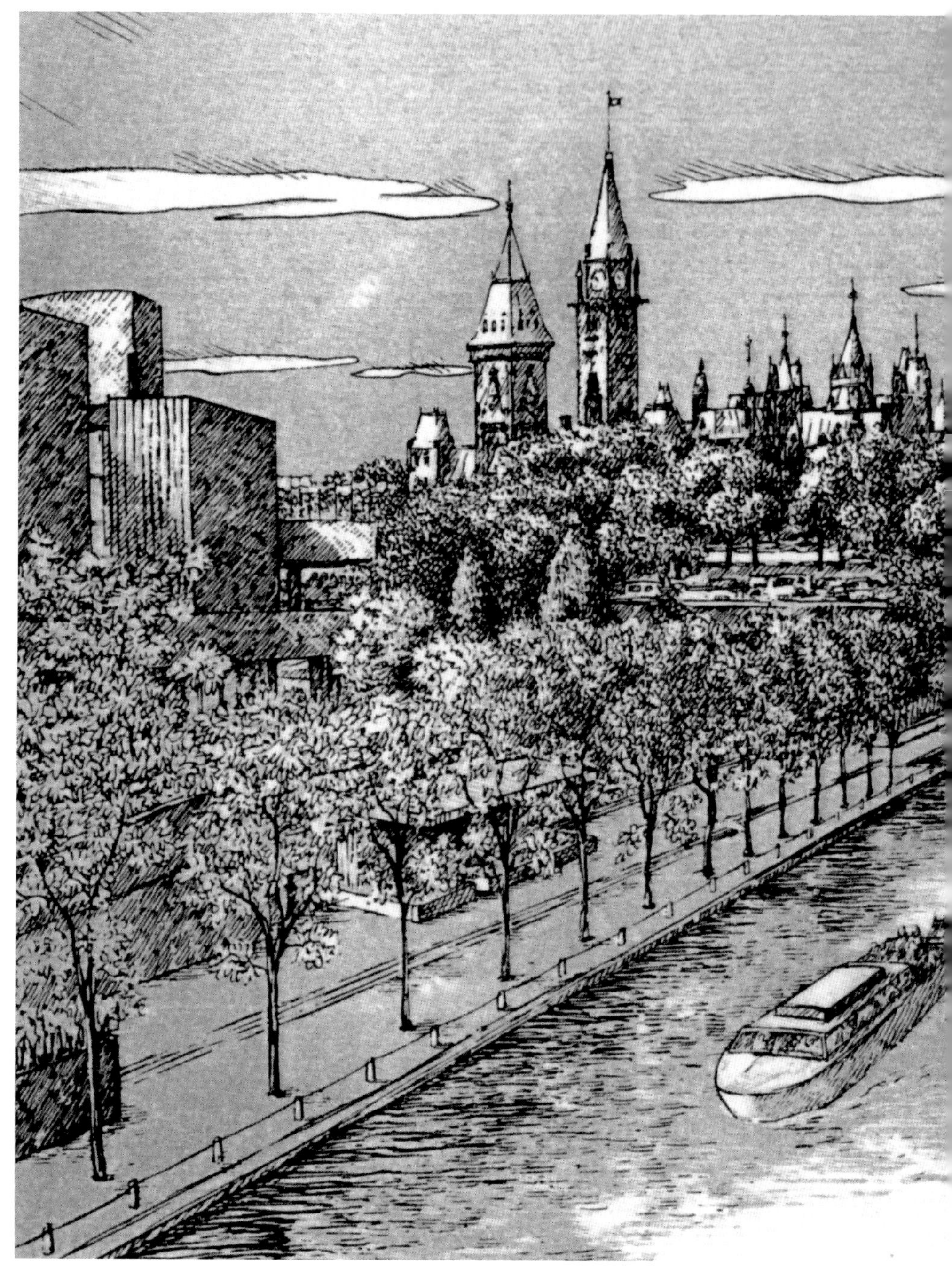

Boating on the Rideau. *Author's collection.*

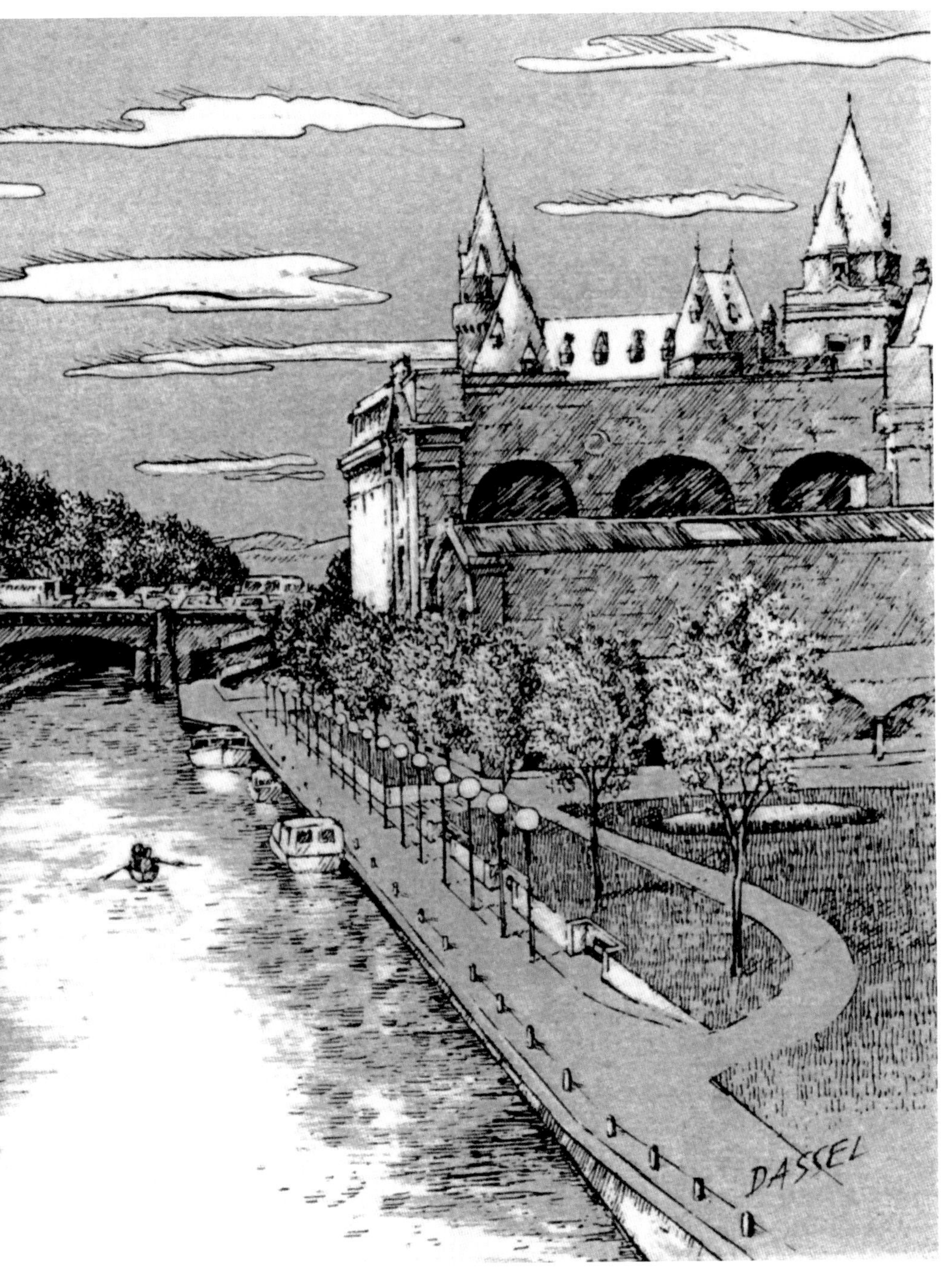
DASSEL

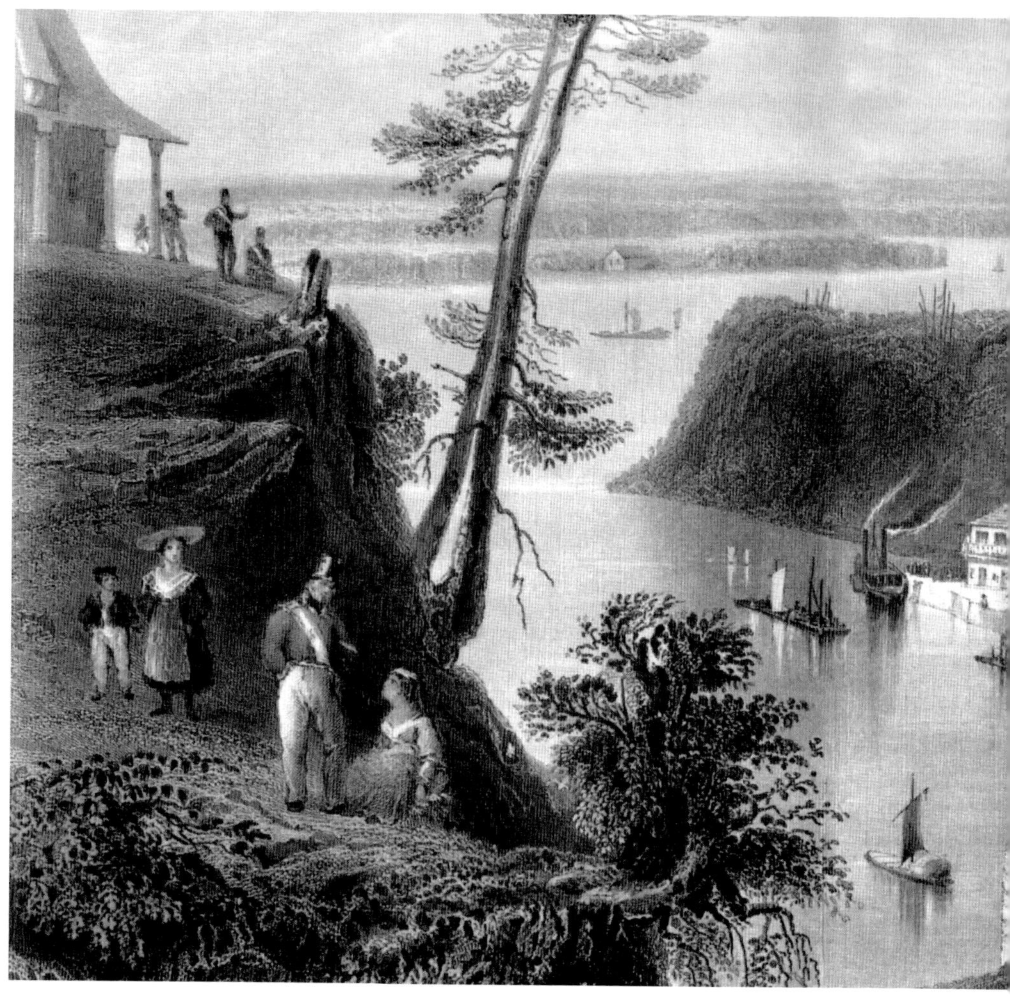

such as railways and trucking. It was also a path for immigration as people filled up the land between Kingston and Ottawa in the 1830s and 1840s. In the 1860s, utilitarian transport gave way to specialized steamers for canal excursions and tourism. Today, in the twenty-first century, the canal is still a principal tourist attraction for boaters, who still come to use the old system and travel between Kingston and Ottawa into either the Ottawa River boating region or to the vast reaches of the Great Lakes—it allows them to avoid the busy traffic of the St. Lawrence system. The use of the early pleasure palaces only declined as the automobile developed and became the preferred means of transportation. A quote from Nelles's study accurately describes the smell of goods travelling the canal: "Flour, sugar, coffee, chests of tea, bags of fine

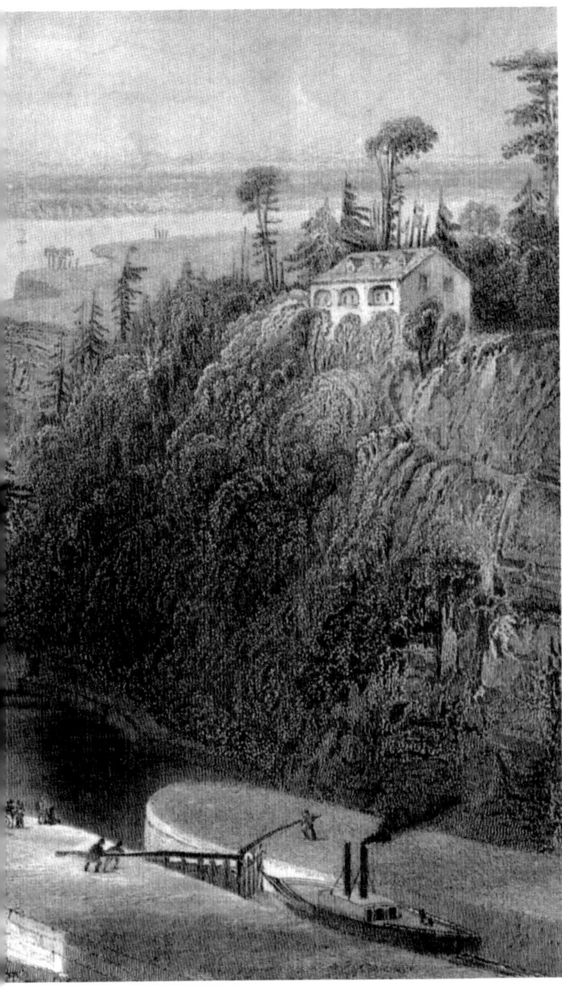

Rideau Canal illustration. *Belden.*

salt, matches, tobacco in caddies and countless boxes of doughnuts. Drugs for the doctors and barrels and kegs of beer and whisky to keep the local innkeepers in stock also came by water." Other varied objects included a blacksmith's anvil, platform scales, pipe organs and cases of glassware, as well as household furniture.

By the 1840s, there were nineteen steamers operating on the Rideau route. In 1848, ninety thousand passengers used the canal (higher than Colonel By's estimate), and competition was fierce among the myriad transportation companies. Passage was limited, and towns along the route were little developed. By the 1850s, the expanding railway system was overshadowing the canal, and the entrepreneurs struggled for business to maintain incomes. At this time, federal authorities debated abandoning the canal forever. For example, only 874 passengers were accommodated in 1874.

The solution led to the age of the excursion steamer, which was first introduced by Moss Kent Dickinson in 1863. He introduced the 110-foot *City of Ottawa*. The boat was lavishly furnished in the hopes of attracting wealthier patrons than the immigrant population that had been using the canal system. The steamer was one of the earliest vessels to include provisions for the comfort of its passengers, including a 90-foot saloon, which considerably raised standards of passenger comfort.

Public patronage picked up in the late 1870s and multiplied during the debut of the *Rideau Belle* in 1885, which "set the climate for the enjoyment of tours and excursions." The steamer made journeys twice weekly between Kingston and Ottawa, taking seventy-six hours to make a round trip. The steamboats now sought a new breed of leisure summer travellers. The public responded enthusiastically, and the new era gave the canal a new lease on life. Canal patronage had increased to 7,500 by 1892, a far cry from the glory days of the 1840s, but it was considerably more comfortable.

The next standard of excellence was the *James Swift*, built in 1893. A quote from the *Rideau Record* in Smith Falls described the ship as being "without doubt the finest that has ever plied the Rideau." Several other increasingly luxurious cruise ships followed the *James Swift*. They contained indoor plumbing, hot and cold running water and other luxuries not found in all but the most elite homes in society. The entrepreneur behind the luxury cruise ships was Captain Daniel Noonan, who launched the Rideau Lakes Navigation Company in 1899 and had even more commodious ships built. The *Swift* was followed by the *Rideau Queen* and the *Rideau King*, which was a rebuilt *James Swift*.

Excursions were organized by parliamentarians and masons. The *Perth Courier* offered a description: "The journey though slow, was a pleasant one, as the scenery was bewitching. Once the locks were passed the boat shot ahead under full steam to the ferry, where about fifty more passengers joined. The most enjoyable part of the trip then began and for about fifteen miles the eye of the traveller gazed on a pretty expansive water and islands and cottages and verdure clad shores." The river steamers were succeeded by many smaller boats—ironically enough, this became one of the reasons for the demise of the canal pleasure steamers. By 1900, the first gasoline launch was afloat on the Rideau system. Increasing popularity and relatively low cost of motorboats were factors, but the death of Captain Noonan in 1914 was the final nail in the coffin. The onset of World War I might have played a part as well. The demise of the Edwardian age saw the end of the canal steamer.

The Rideau Canal proved its worth over the years, although never for the purpose for which it was designed. Its time in the golden age of the 1840s saw it used for pure transportation for pleasure steamers and recreation motorboats. Even today, more than 180 years after it was opened, the canal caters to many pleasure boats every year and still operates as it did on the day it opened.

OTTAWA'S STREET RAILWAYS: THE LIFE AND DEATH OF AN URBAN TRANSIT SYSTEM

With all the growth in our city in the past fifty years, I wonder how many people remember the days when you took a streetcar from, among other routes, the old train station out to Rideau and Charlotte. Thanks to University of Ottawa professor Don Davis's work in *Ottawa: Making a Capital*, we have a detailed history of the streetcar system, how it grew and how it was eventually done away with.

Ottawa's street railway system died in 1959 after a life of sixty-eight years. Did citizens love or hate the system? Davis noted that the appreciation for the system was like some marriages—initial high enthusiasm followed by many years of declining interest, given our rapidly changing technological world. Perhaps the streetcar era has lessons to teach in the consideration of expanded light rail.

The new streetcar system was opened on June 29, 1891, largely as a result of the work of two local entrepreneurs, Thomas Aherne and William Soper. Everyone thought that such a project would fail because of Ottawa's winters. However, at the time, unless you could afford a horse and buggy, plus a sleigh in the winter, there was no way to get around the growing city except by walking. The system proved to be an immediate success, even in the winter. The system had the first electrically heated cars in Canada, maybe even in the world. The Ottawa Car Manufacturing Company made streetcars that were exported to other parts of Canada. In the early days of the system, ridership rose seven times faster than the population. In 1921, at the peak of the system's success, each citizen took an average of 336 rides per year. The fares were low—about three tickets for ten cents. Despite attempts at updating and revival, Ottawa's Street Railway went steadily downhill from this point.

Public love for the automobile was probably a contributing factor, as were the rising costs of maintenance, expansion of the roadbed and new streetcar technology. The investors also played a part, as they took an increasing amount of dividends out of the system and did not develop a good reserve fund for necessary expansion and repairs. By 1924, automobiles were using up the spaces needed for transit cars. They blocked the progress of streetcars by parking on city streets, forcing other cars to drive on the track allowance and stopping to pick up passengers and make left turns. The streetcar trips became longer. Davis pointed out that "trains in 1956 were slower than they have been in 1901. Downtown it was faster to walk."

Having made money for years, the owners of the Ottawa Electric Railway (OER) now wanted to sell the system to the city. While the city council was willing to buy, assuming it would have a monopoly on inner-city transit, plebiscites were rejected four times over a five-year period up until 1929. The taxpayers did not want to pay. In January 1924, the city and the OER reached an agreement to extend the service for five years, subject to renewal in 1929. This agreement created more problems than it solved. First, the car fare was frozen at five cents per ride, lower than nearly all other North American systems, and the five-year term was not conducive to the kind of capital investment that was becoming increasingly necessary. Thanks to the increasing competition from the automobile, streets became even more clogged and streetcar trips even longer. In 1929, it was apparent that new equipment was necessary, and the five-year contract emboldened the owners to buy new equipment with borrowed money. Contracts were met, and then came October 1929. Pressure for loan payment became intense, but the fare was still frozen at five cents, so when authority was finally obtained to raise the fare to seven cents, ridership dropped by 16 percent despite the revenue increase of 10 percent. The OER staggered on until the end of World War II, but the writing was on the wall. Revenues could never match increasing costs of new equipment, track extensions, competition from the auto industry and various interest groups.

For example, Glebe residents would not permit streetcar routes along residential streets. The forerunners of the National Capital Commission (NCC) did not want unsightly power lines overhead, and riders demanded more comfortable and more frequent service. The federal government increased business taxes enormously during the Second World War. Trams were crowded and noisy—people preferred buses before the negative environmental effects of buses were discovered. Despite the eventual creation of the Ottawa Transit Commission in 1947–48, these questions continued, and new ones arose. The shutdown of the system was obvious, as too many groups wanted the tram lines to disappear. By 1958–59, the pressures had become too much, and the old streetcar lines were removed. The only mourners at the time were those of the older populations, who had fond memories of the great days of the street railways that happened before and during World War I.

THE SKATING RINKS OF OTTAWA

With Winterlude being such a popular annual festival, where attendants can skate on the largest skating rink in the world, it's a fitting historical subject to summarize the use of skating rinks in Ottawa. People have been officially skating on the Rideau Canal since 1982, but the idea to have skating rinks in Ottawa has been around for much longer. We have Paul Kitchen to thank for painstakingly researching old newspapers and land records to bring us a history of hockey rinks and, in the process, let us know about other uses for those hockey rinks.

The first formal skating rink in Ottawa was opened in 1868. In the years between 1884 and 1927, there were three different locations that went by the name "Dey's Rink." These were all the rinks managed by the Dey brothers, and their history is fascinating, especially some of the things that happened in the three rinks. Some things are part of hockey history in Canada, and others are stories of a purely local nature. Each rink, in turn, served as the home base of the Ottawa Hockey Club, known variously as the Ottawas, the Silver Seven and the Senators.

In 1923, the club moved to the auditorium that stood where the YMCA/YWCA stands now. I remember the old auditorium from 1962, when it was the scene of an event that warmed the Cold War a little: the Red Army Chorus performed there, and it was magnificent!

In 1868, the Ottawa Skating and Curling Club opened the "Royal," located on Slater Street just east of Elgin. In 1884, the club even installed electric lighting, then in the experimental stage. The *Ottawa Citizen* of December 20, 1884, announced that the new rink, operated by the Dey brothers, would open on Saturday afternoon at 2:30 p.m. Members of the Governor-General's Foot Guards would provide music. Very close to the Royal, this first Dey brothers arena was located on the east side of the Rideau Canal, near the Maria (now Laurier) Street foot bridge. It had a high, curved roof and was 200 feet long by 99 feet wide. It boasted heated dressing rooms, electric lighting and a rink that was about a 150- by 60-foot rectangle. It became very popular in the last decades of the nineteenth century and featured many skating carnivals and masquerades. However, by the fall of 1895, the rink had made way for the tracks and depot of the Canadian Atlantic Railway.

The Dey brothers took advantage of the new Ottawa Electric Railway and moved their operation to the "boonies" of the day: at the North West corner

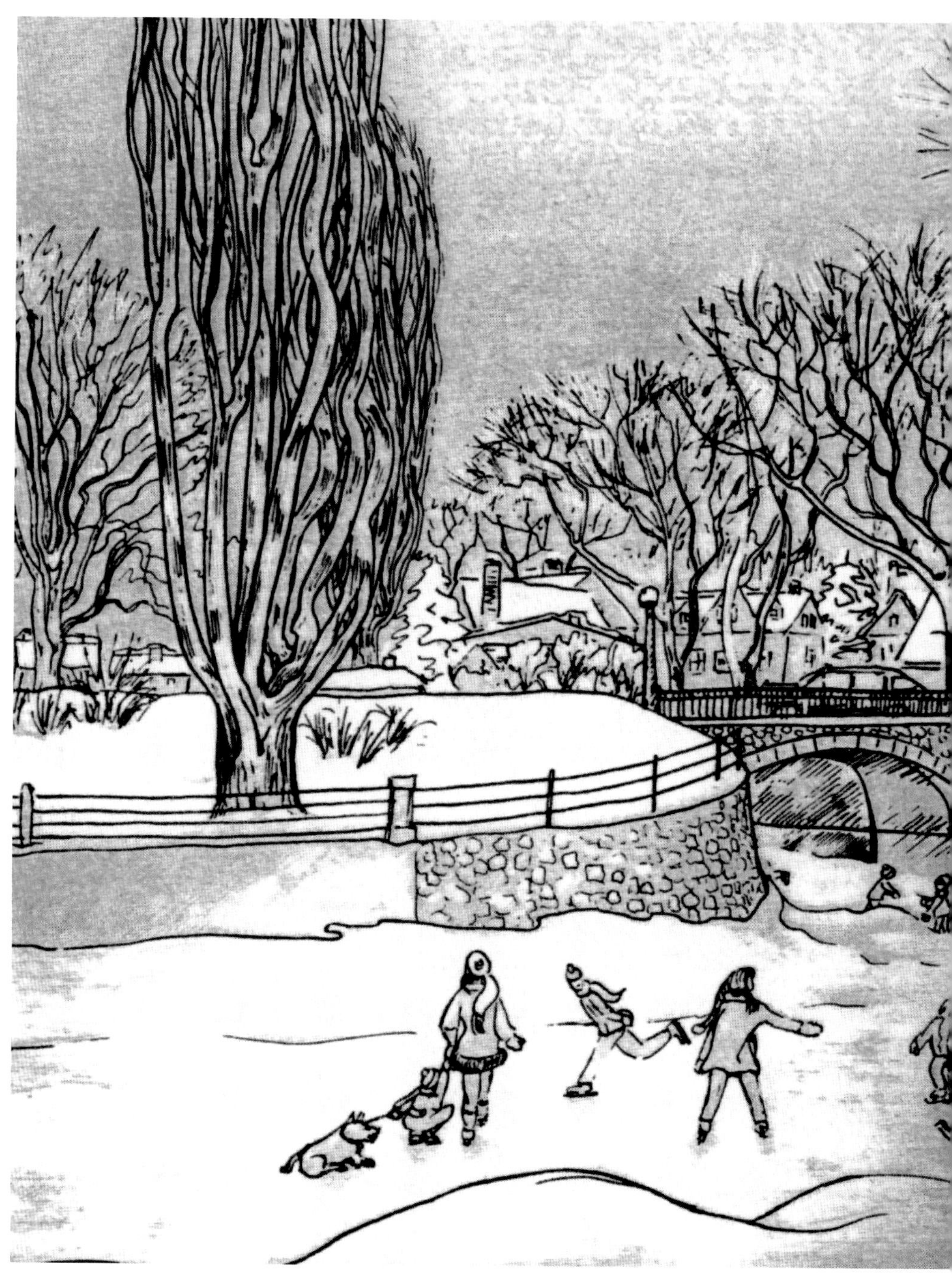

Skating on the Rideau Canal. *Author's collection.*

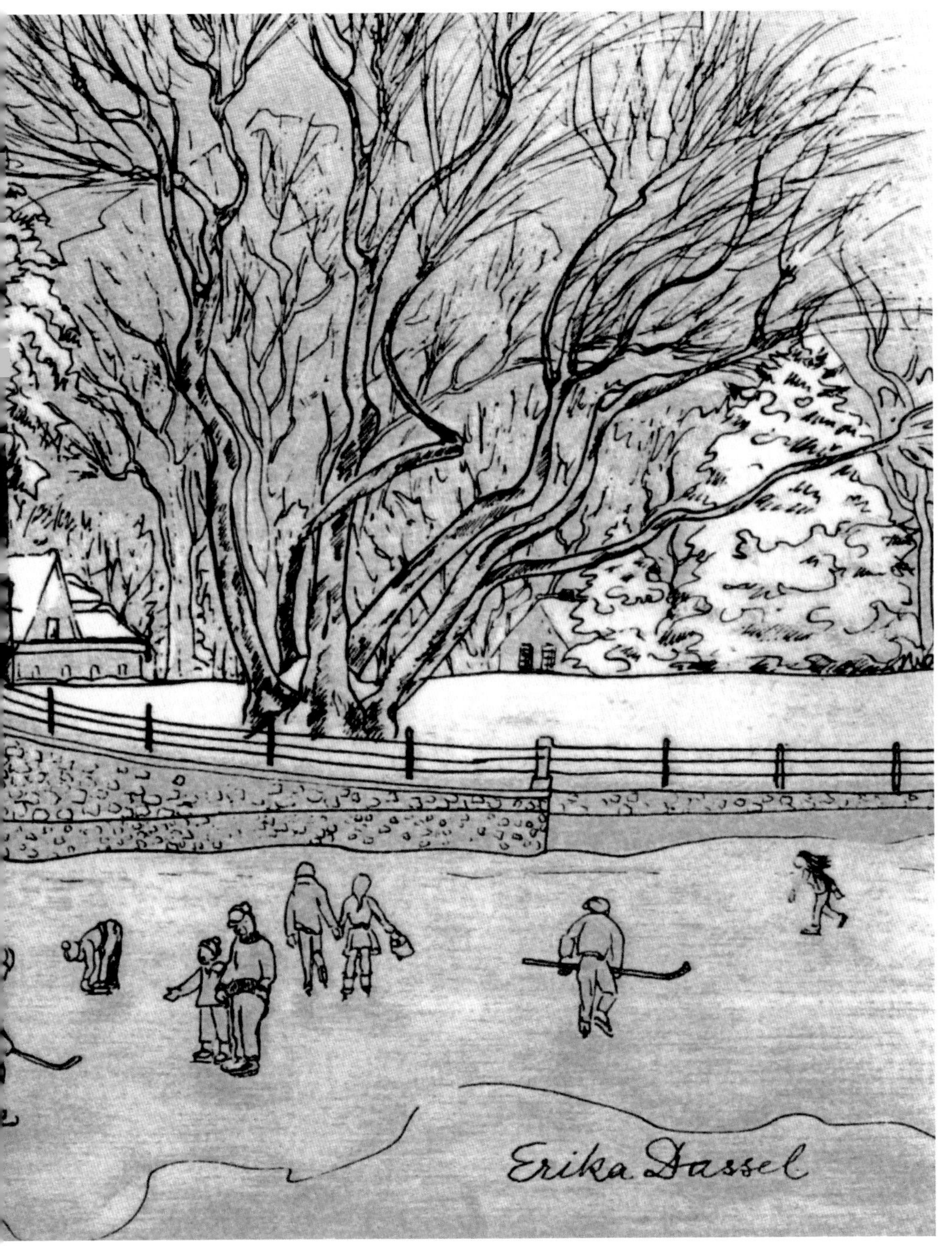
Erika Dassel

of Gladstone (then Ann Street) and Bay. They acquired several lots for $2,450. They built a rink that was meant to be used for hockey. The natural ice surface measured 81 by 200 feet, said by the *Citizen* to be the largest in Canada at that time. The new rink opened on December 17, 1896, and admission was fifteen cents for adults and ten cents for children. From then until the end of the 1907 hockey season, the rink was very popular—patrons arrived by foot, the electric railway and horse-drawn sleigh. It was in this rink that the fabled two-game series between Ottawa's Silver Seven and the Dawson City Klondikers took place in January 1905. The Dawson City club lost by wide margins, but the players had travelled some four thousand miles to the games, so perhaps they were tired.

The next and final rink operated by the Deys was built in the summer and fall of 1907 on land on Laurier Avenue leased for twenty years for $166.66 per month from Ms. Esther Sherwood. One of the conditions of the lease was that an aesthetic contribution to the nation's capital would be built on the land. The new rink was hardly that. On the north side of the arena was a large ad for the Dey brothers' boat works just across the canal.

On the night of January 11, 1908, the Ottawa Senators opened their first season in the new rink by defeating the Montreal Wanderers, 12–2, in front of a crowd estimated at 7,500 people. The next fifteen years saw the Ottawa club claim the Stanley Cup five times.

By 1922, pressure was on for more arena space, and the debate raged over where to place a new auditorium that was to seat at least five thousand people in the hockey stands and up to ten thousand for other events. It would be the first rink in Ottawa to have artificial ice—the 1920 Stanley Cup games had to be moved to Toronto because the ice melted in Ottawa. Finally constructed at the corner of Argyll and O'Connor, the new auditorium brought the city into more modern days. The older rinks were replaced by the relatively modern auditorium.

In 1927, the old Laurier site was sold by Ms. Sherwood to the Federal District Commission for $60,000. Prime Minister Mackenzie King was said to have had a hand in getting rid of the old rink, as it really wasn't appropriate for a national capital improvement. He would probably be amazed at today's world.

Today, we have the "Rink of Dreams," which opened on the grounds of city hall so skating aficionados could pursue their favourite winter sport. The surface is smoother than the natural ice on the canal, even if the surface is considerably smaller. Prime Minister King might have felt that this was too plebeian a use for the grounds of the centre of municipal government.

MAPPING CANADA

One of the things Ottawa has contributed to Canada has been the forging of the maps that fostered the nation's growth. From the early nineteenth century to the present day, on foot, horseback and by aircraft, geologists, surveyors and the Royal Canadian Air Force flying modified Lancaster bombers have gone from one coast to another to produce maps and charts that other travellers and explorers, mining companies and military engineers (to name just a few) have used for the benefit of all.

The Geological Survey of Canada, which has been based in Ottawa since 1881, began the process even before the organization moved to Ottawa; it continued the process for many years while based in the city, sending out exploration parties each summer. The GSC published the first *Atlas of Canada*, even though it had vast areas as yet unexplored. Major work was done by the RCAF crews based at Rockliffe Airport from 1948 to 1964. Many of those who attended the Musical ride in those days can't forget the sounds of a Lancaster only about one hundred feet above them, roaring overhead as it set off on a mission to northern Canada.

The Geological Survey produced literally hundreds of reports on the physical characteristics of minerals, plants and animals long before Canadians even recognized them. Many of the places that are very remote in Canada were named after the explorers responsible for the survey. However, the exploration—based on travel made by canoe, horseback or on foot—had serious limitations when you consider the distances that had to be travelled or the vast areas to be covered. It remained for the age of aircraft to complete the tasks so that the whole of the second-largest country in the world was mapped and surveyed by the early 1960s, and mostly by the aircraft that were based in Ottawa.

The real impetus for aircraft surveys came from the Cold War. Defensive radar was needed to both detect incoming bombers and guide interceptors to them. Two major radar lines were involved: the Pinetree Line, along the fifty-fifth parallel, and the Dew Line, along the continental margin. Maps to guide the aircraft were few and far between, and those that did exist had little detailed information to guide the aircrews. "Photo" aircraft were required to fly at altitudes near twenty thousand feet on oxygen for up to twelve hours on a stretch. Other aircraft surveyed the land using a form of short-range radar called SHORAN, which could fix positions with an accuracy of one foot over a distance of two hundred miles. The high-altitude aircraft of the time were supported by Canso amphibians, which flew into remote lakes and whose crews trudged up to a high spot to install the radar stations; two men would live in these places for weeks on end, manning the radar sets so that the aircraft would get the signals necessary to complete the surveys. It was a lonely existence living off rations and surrounded by blackflies. It was a job well done and worthy of our respect today.

Forward bases for the aircraft were located at such places as Goose Bay, Whitehorse and Resolute Bay in the high arctic. This work was completed without a single lost aircraft or man. Maintenance crews worked around the clock in short summers to keep the aircraft flying. The whole exercise was awarded the McKee Trophy for Aeronautical Excellence, given to Wing Commander Jack Showler (lieutenant colonel by today's nomenclature), commanding officer of the squadron involved (408 P Squadron). Today, the unit flies helicopters in such places as Afghanistan, the Philippines and Haiti—just one of Canada's proud military traditions. Many of the squadron members still call Ottawa their home, and the city has every reason to be proud of an accomplishment that aided Canada, especially in otherwise unexplored areas of the country.

Her Honour, the Mayor

No book on Ottawa would be complete without a few words on Charlotte Elizabeth Whitton, the first female mayor of a significant city in Canada. Born at the end of the nineteenth century in Renfrew, Ontario, Charlotte graduated from Queen's University in Kingston with academic honours, but she was also well known in the sports circles at Queen's. She was a forerunner of Canadian women's hockey glory at the Olympics; she was the star of the university women's hockey team and was reputed to be the fastest skater in her league. She was also the first female editor of the *Queen's Journal*, in 1917.

She went on to champion children's welfare and founded the beginnings of current organizations such as the Canadian Council on Social Development. She was a staunch nationalist who disliked the present Canadian flag and some of the other options developed under Prime Minister Pearson. She first became mayor of Ottawa in 1951 upon the sudden death of her predecessor, Grenville Goodwin. She had been elected as a city councillor

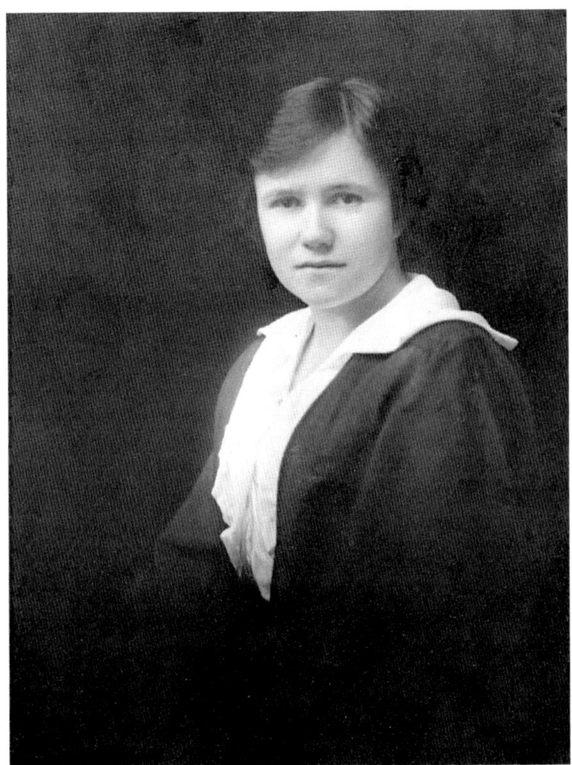

Left: A young Charlotte Whitton, future mayor, as a student at Queen's University. *National Archives of Canada.*

Below: Mayor Charlotte Whitton receiving an award.

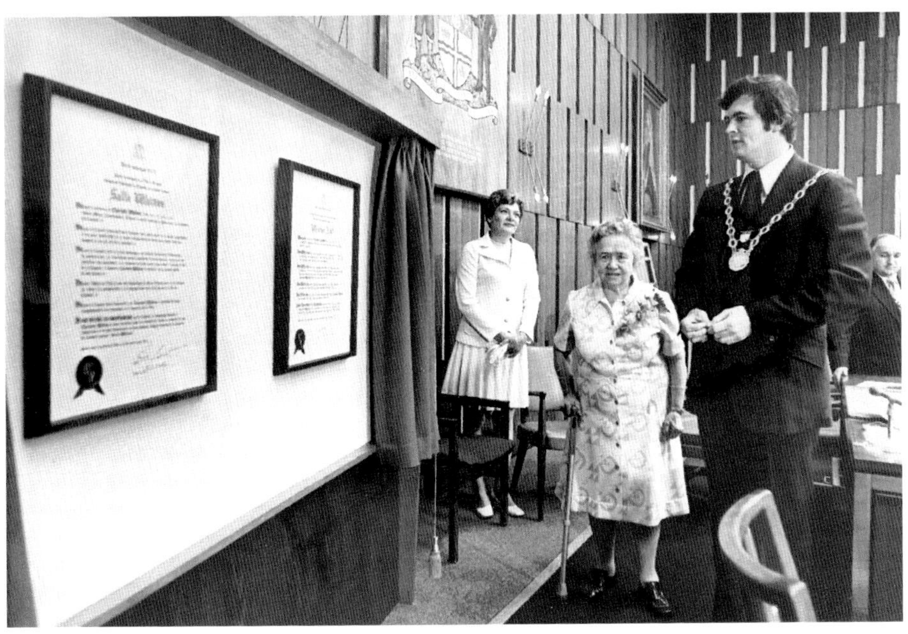

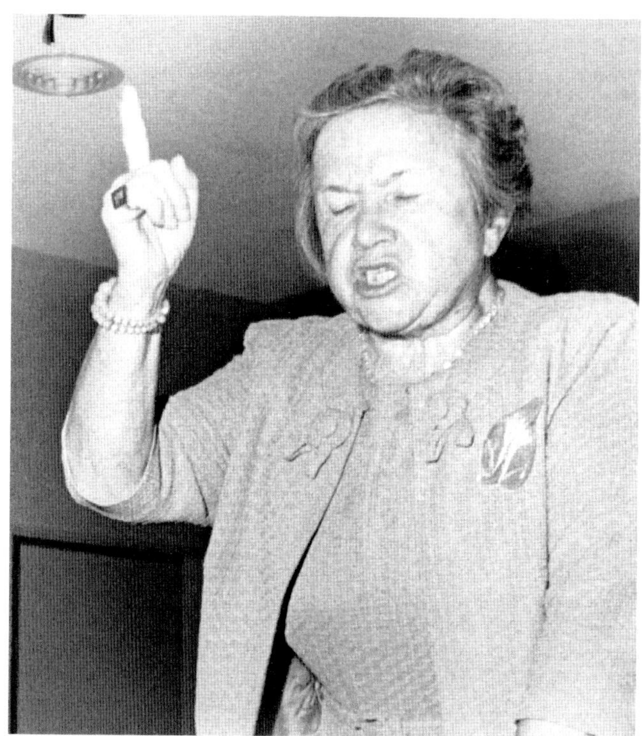

Left: Charlotte in full flight! *Ottawa City Archives.*

Below: Charlotte with Pierre Benoit.

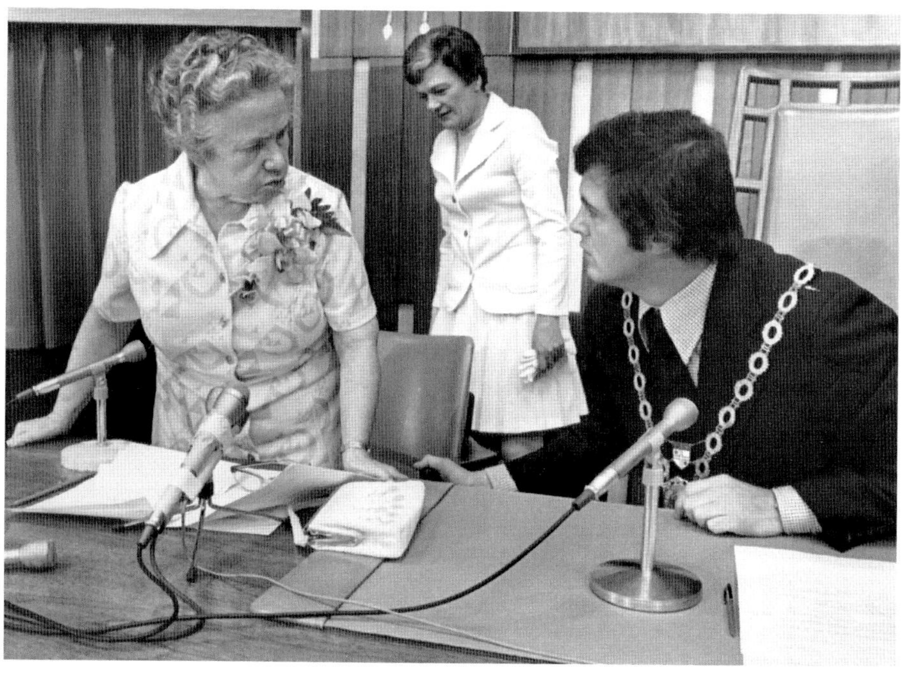

but was acclaimed as mayor by all the councillors elected along with her. She was famous for one comment that became a classic feminist quote: "Whatever women do they must do twice as well as men to be thought half as good. Luckily, this is not difficult." Her first term ended in 1956, but she went on to serve a second term from 1960 to 1964. During both terms, she was a steadfast defender of Canadian traditions and called Pearson's three-maple-leaf vision of the Canadian flag a symbol of cowardice because it didn't include the red ensign. After she retired in 1964, she was made an officer of the Order of Canada in 1967.

Some of her actions stirred up controversies that are still topics of discussion today. She was accused of being anti-Semitic, largely based on two incidents, and it became known that she had had a continuing relationship with another woman named Margaret Grier. This did not become public knowledge until 1999, more than two decades after Miss Whitton died. To this day, no one is certain exactly what the relationship was. Miss Whitton has been called anti-Semitic because of two incidents in her distinguished career. The first incident involved her queries about the wisdom of allowing Jewish and Armenian children to come to Canada shortly before World War II. In 1938, she showed opposition to the idea. She was at a conference to create the Canadian National Committee on Refugees, and the comments she made were interpreted as evidence she was anti-Jewish, with particular reference to children. At the same time, she was the chair of the Canadian Council on Child Welfare, and her arguments may well have been taken out of context. She may simply have been concerned about the allocation of responsibility for a possible flood of child refugees.

The second incident triggering such claims was due to her reluctance to allow Mr. Bertram Loeb to contribute $500,000 to the Ottawa Civic Hospital and have his name appear on the building. One author has stated that Whitton was such an Anglophile that she didn't want to face the changing character of Canadian society. In 2011, amid controversy, the city decided not to place her name on the new city archives building. Despite this, Miss Whitton contributed to the best of her intelligence and ability to a growing city and stands out as a figure to be remembered.

Part VII
The Past in the Present

Ottawa's Ghost Stories

Are you one of those people who likes Stephen King stories or tales of places that are haunted? The historical structures in central Ottawa offer their share of ghostly anecdotes.

Let's start with the oldest stone building in Ottawa, now known as the Bytown Museum. It dates back to 1827, when it was Colonel John By's commissariat (or warehouse) while the canal was being built. In those long-ago days, we didn't have banks or ATMs. Worker payrolls and contractor funds had to be brought aboard ship and were stored in the commissariat until needed.

Naturally, some people thought that it would be an easy target for a little grand theft, but they had to get past Duncan McNabb, who was in charge of protecting the gold and silver. Duncan must have done his job well as there is no record of any theft from the storehouse. Perhaps he is still doing it to this day, as workers at the museum swear that they have heard footsteps following them up the stairs or heard the same footsteps when they are alone in the museum. At night, modern motion detectors are triggered when there is no one in the museum. One ex-employee swore that whenever Duncan's name was spoken, the sales computer went crazy. Some people think that Duncan is still there, living in the treasury crypt and guarding the money.

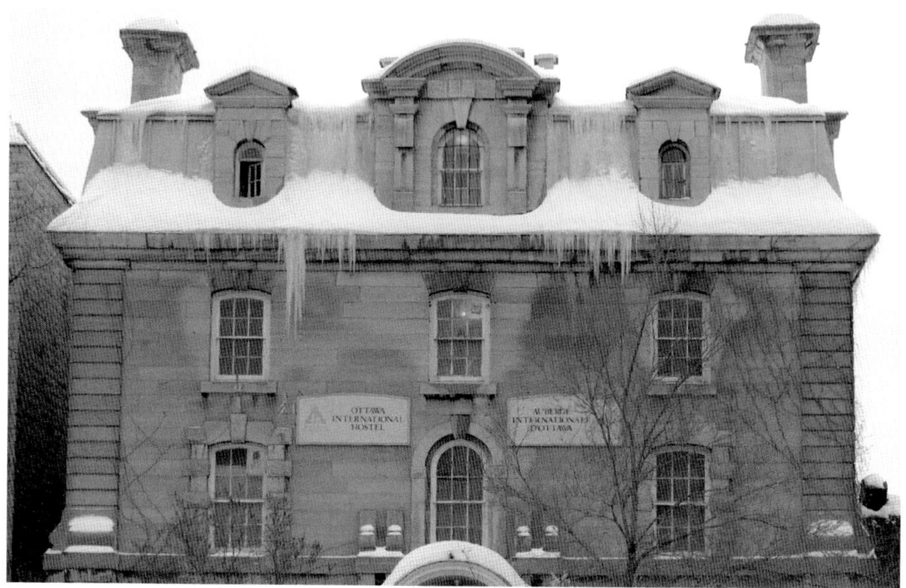

Old city gaol—the perhaps haunted site of Patrick Whelan's execution and burial.

Ask the people at the building that is now Friday's Roast Beef House on Elgin Street, originally built as a doctor's home in 1875, about the strange goings-on at a particular table on the second floor, and you'll hear another chilling story. People sitting at this particular table have felt the proverbial icy breeze, and things on their table have been moved even when no one is there. I once mustered my courage and took my wife to dinner there, but we didn't feel anything except the stares of other guests at other tables who were waiting for something to happen. The good doctor who owned the house also had a hospital in his home, so no one is quite sure who or what the spirit represents.

Across the street, look into the old main entrance to the former Ottawa Teacher's College, now part of city hall, and you might see the ghost of the "Grey Lady" come out of one door and go into another. Certain politicians and city staff swear that they have seen her. There are several stories about how she got there and what she is up to, but we can be sure that she is not one of Ottawa's past lady mayors, as she is dressed in nineteenth-century clothes, or so the story goes. She is probably some past teacher who keeps coming back to collect a last homework assignment.

The final ghost to be mentioned here haunts the old city jail, or gaol, as it used to be spelled. Authorities used to hang people in that jail, so you can take your pick of any number of potentially unsettled spirits. D'Arcy

McGee, a Father of Confederation, was murdered, and Patrick Whelan, a former Fenian, was convicted and hanged for this crime. Many people think that the gaol ghost is Whelan himself, still protesting that he is innocent of the crime. Others feel that the ghost might be the prisoner whose testimony was used to convict Whelan, doomed to haunt the jail forever because he lied (and perhaps got some benefit from his testimony), but the process may have led to the execution of an innocent man. We'll never know for sure.

There are many haunted places here, far too many to mention. On a misty summer or autumn evening, join the ghost walkers under the bear statue at the end of Sparks Street for a Haunted Walk of Ottawa. You might be led by a lady dressed in black and carrying a flickering torch. Some of the ghosts you might meet were part of this story. Of course, if the night is misty, with no moon, it can get even more interesting.

Old Buildings Left Behind

Part of this series of Ottawa in the "old days" will be to tell you about buildings that have been around for a long time. There is an active organization called Heritage Ottawa that specializes in commemorating older buildings in the capital city. It teams up with the city every year in May to make building tours available to anyone interested. The event is called Doors Open Ottawa, and many interesting facets of both old and modern Ottawa are presented. If architecture and our relatively ancient buildings (for Canada) are of interest, Heritage Ottawa has a wonderful collection of information at its disposal. Some of us even call it the "Building Protective Society" of Ottawa.

Many passersby on the Mackenzie King Bridge or those driving up Nicolas Street wonder what the old, rectangular building across the street from the old city jail represents. It has been featured in several of the Doors Open Ottawa events and has a very interesting and checkered history. Owned now by the people who own the Rideau Centre, it began life in 1873 as the City Registry Office, where all official records of the city were kept. If you needed to know the history of a piece of land or building together with who owned or had owned it, you had to go the City Registry Office. All official records of Bytown and the City of Ottawa were kept there. Inside the building is a unique set of rails, now covered, that allowed cast-iron shelving to be moved back and forth as if on railway tracks.

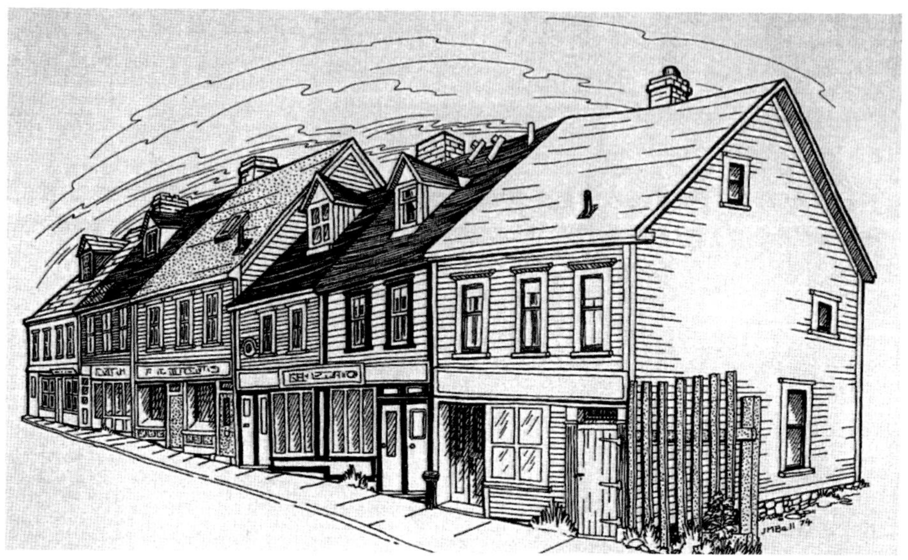

Examples of some of the earlier town houses. *Author's collection.*

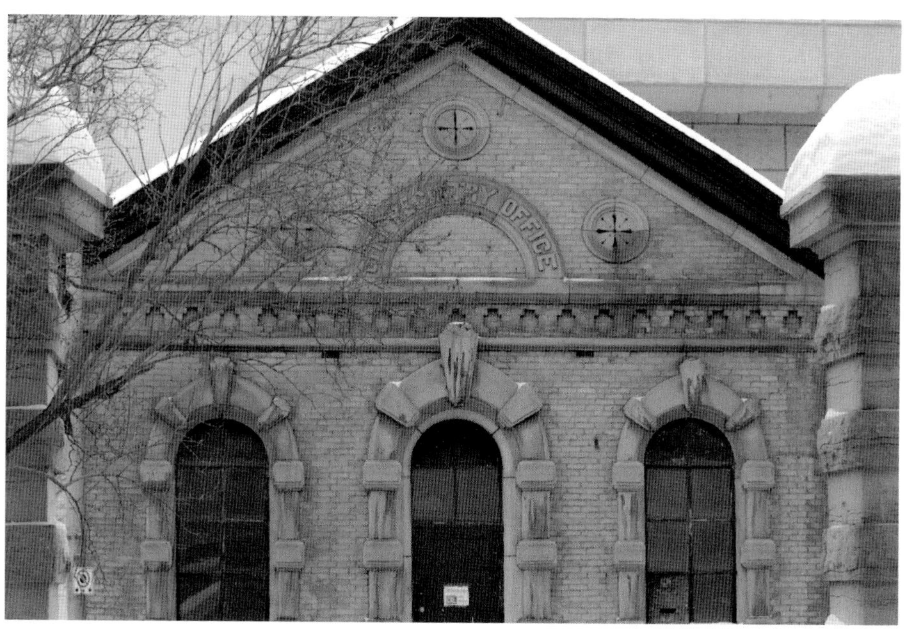

The deserted old registry office built in 1873 *Author's collection.*

When you first enter the building, you go into what was the office, where the clerks would take information or draw files from the storage room, which was next when walking through the building. After passing through the file storage area, there were a number of small offices, much smaller than today's offices. There is one small bathroom and a storage closet. The whole building was heated by a potbellied stove burning wood and coal that the clerks had to keep running. You can imagine what it was like on a cold winter day! In 1910, the registry office needed to be expanded, so a brand-new one was built. This replacement is no longer with us, and the aforementioned files are now at the city hall. The original registry office is still standing, and the replacement one is long gone.

This building has had a number of uses over the years, not the least of which was to function as the original Bytown Museum from 1917 until 1951. The historical society, founded in 1898 as the Women's Historical Society of Ottawa, needed space for its growing collection of artifacts and convinced the city fathers of the time that the old registry office would make an ideal museum. The "railway tracks" of the file shelves were covered over with exhibits of things like Colonel By's furniture. After 1951, the museum moved to its present quarters in the old commissariat building beside the locks of the Rideau Canal.

The old registry office has very solid twelve-foot-deep foundations, which were built to prevent thievery of critical landownership records via tunneling. These foundations have served other purposes over the years. This building was also a legal office at one time, as well as home of the Tourist and Convention Bureau of Ottawa. It sat, cold and deserted and damp, until it was opened for Doors Open Ottawa. Many people wonder what is going to happen to it next. The Rideau Centre owners have talked about expanding the shopping mall, and the old building would be in the way of such an expansion. We will have to wait to see what transpires, but one alternative would be to encase the old building in the expansion and thereby keep alive a piece of the city's heritage. Another alternative would be to move the building to another site. There are probably other ideas that readers can think of, but the economic issues might determine just when we will lose the familiar landmark. Only the future, not the past, will tell.

Some questions and answers of note: (1) When did the old registry office become the Bytown Museum? (Answer: 1917.); (2) How deep are its foundations? (Answer: twelve feet.); and (3) What purposes has the building served? (Answer: museum, legal office and headquarters for the Ottawa Tourist and Convention Bureau.)

As mentioned, the old registry office was built in 1873. There are even older buildings around Ottawa, and many of them can be seen in a quick trip around Lower Town and Sandy Hill. A cluster of them is viewable near the Basilica at Sussex and St. Patrick. The Basilica itself is one of the oldest surviving structures in Ottawa.

The oldest of all Ottawa buildings is the Bytown Museum, located beside the canal. Built in 1826, this building was used as Colonel By's storehouse for the construction of the Rideau Canal. The canal was opened about 180 years ago, in 1832. Houses were built in Lower Town as the community grew, and in the era when Canada developed into a nation, many upscale houses were built in Sandy Hill. I want to focus on a few of these houses, but a good walking tour would be beneficial to those who want to see even more.

There is a particularly well-preserved house at 138 St. Patrick Street that belonged to Flavien Rochon. Built circa 1832, it is typical of a workingman's home of the era. Before it became the property of Mr. Rochon, four Sisters of the Grey Nuns of the Cross (now the Sisters of Charity of Ottawa) lived there from 1845 to 1851. Mr. Rochon was a carpenter by trade who also sculpted wood, and he was involved in the construction of both Notre Dame Basilica and the Parliamentary Library. The house was acquired by the National Capital Commission in 1965. His next-door neighbour at 142 St. Patrick Street was Dr. Francis Xavier Valade, whose imposing house was built circa 1864. The Valade house is typical of an ancestral home in Normandy. Dr. Valade, who lived there from 1866 to 1918, was one of Ottawa's first doctors and was also one of the doctors responsible for examining Louis Riel before Riel's 1885 trial in Regina. The house was known as Le Balcon Blanc because of the white veranda overhanging the entrance. The original balcony was replaced at the beginning of the nineteenth century.

Before leaving Lower Town for Sandy Hill, I should mention Notre Dame Basilica, the oldest church in the capital, built between 1841 and 1865 on the site of an earlier church built in 1832. It contains beautiful woodwork carved by Louis Philippe Herbert, Phillipe Pariseau and Flavien Rochon. The tower of the Basilica stands nearly fifty-five meters high, and the organ has more than four thousand pipes. This is just a small sample of buildings constructed before Canada became a nation in 1867.

Louis Besserer, a lawyer from Quebec, bought a large parcel of land that became the area known as Sandy Hill, one of the first "elite" neighbourhoods in Ottawa. Besserer purchased the land in 1828, but the area did not really develop before Ottawa was picked as the site of Canada's capital by Queen Victoria in 1857. Growth accelerated after

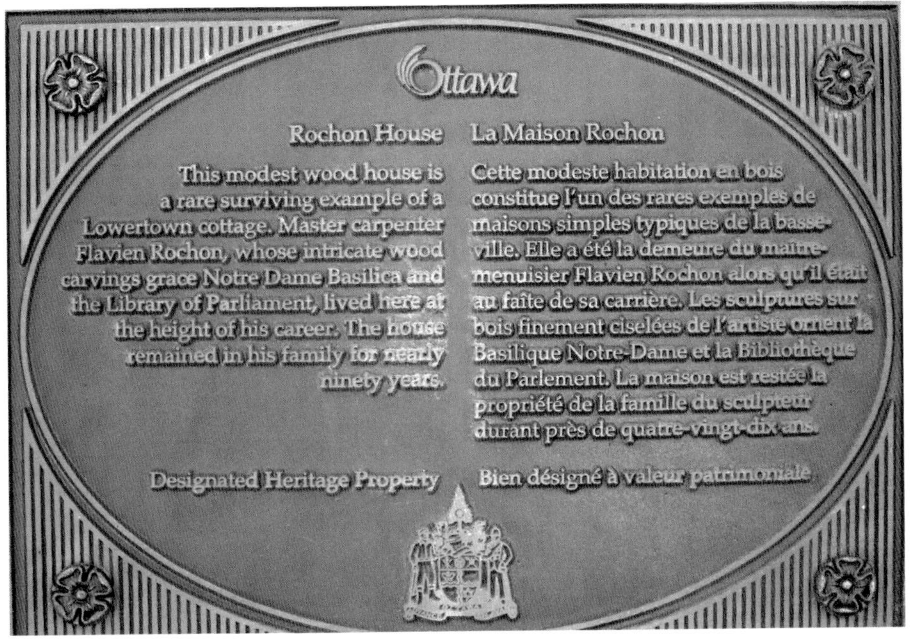

Rochon House plaque. *Author's collection.*

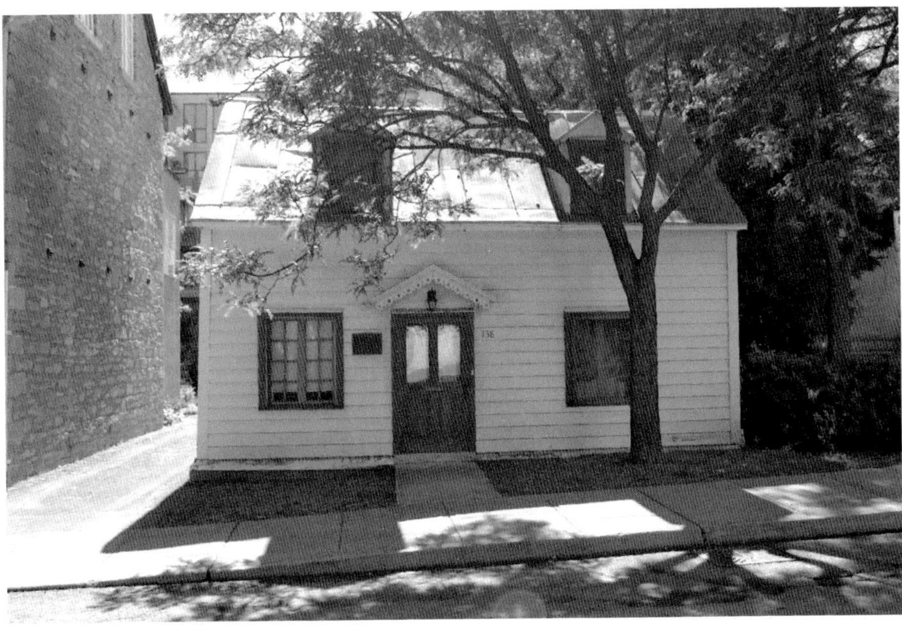

The oldest surviving worker's house in Ottawa dates to 1842. *Author's collection.*

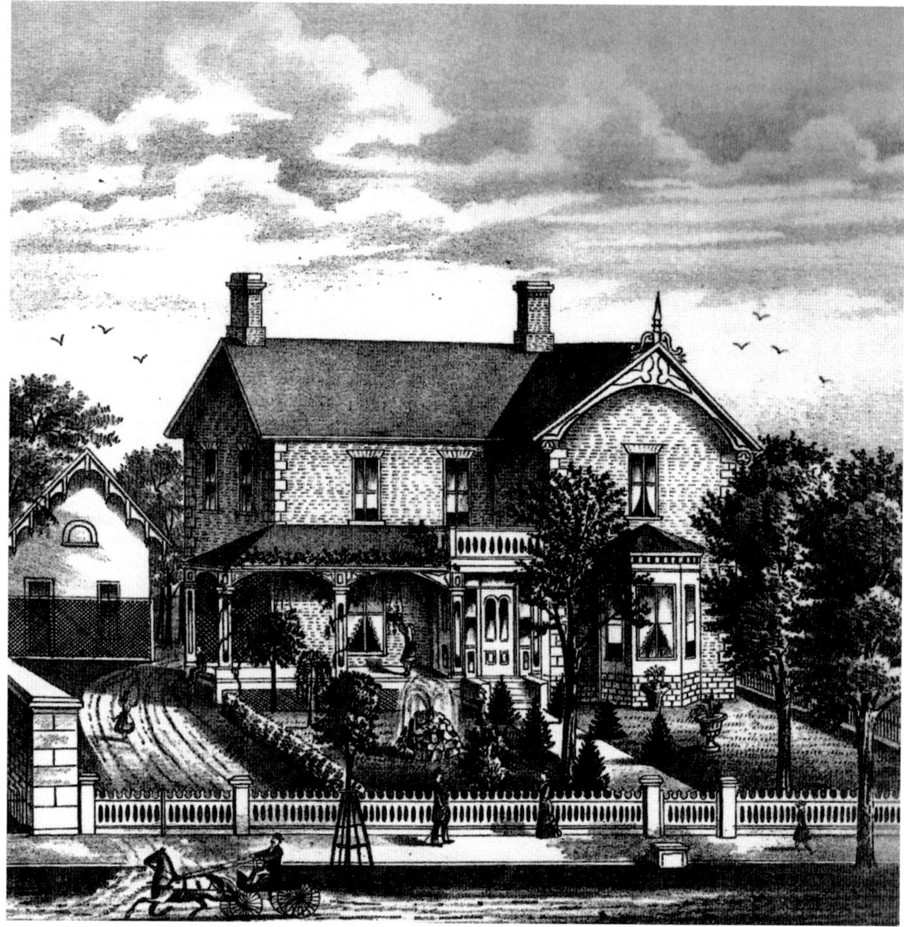

Early mayor's residence in Ottawa. *Belden.*

Confederation, and the area became home to many politicians and senior government officials.

One of the oldest houses in Sandy Hill is the Besserer House, built circa 1844, where L.T. Besserer lived until 1866. It was later occupied by W.T. McDougal, one of the fathers of Confederation. The house is located at 149 Daly Avenue and is really at the centre of Sandy Hill development. Some changes to the verandas and the western face have taken place since 1844, but the house is still largely the same as when it was originally built.

Another older house is the Lyon House, built about 1850. Its first occupant was Robert Fellowes, a son of the original builder, Colonel George Lyon

Fellowes. Robert was a member of Parliament and, in 1876, the mayor of Ottawa. The pamphlet put together by the Regroupement des Organismes du Patrimoine Franco-Ontarienne (ROPFO) notes that "the bay window, the magnificent wooden portico and the decorative flourishes on the façade make it one of the most charming residences."

The Toller House was built circa 1875. Its first occupant, T. Fournier, was a creator of the Supreme Court of Canada and one of the first justices. The next occupant (and the man for whom the house is named) was Fredrick Toller, auditor general of Canada. The next occupant was Louis-Phillipe Brodeur, who was simultaneously minister of finance and of oceans, a justice of the Supreme Court and lieutenant governor of Quebec. One can only guess how he managed to handle all four jobs. The City of Ottawa designated the house a historic property in 1982.

These are only a few of the historic building found in downtown Ottawa. Take a tour under the auspices of ROPFO or Heritage Ottawa and discover much more!

Naming the Corktown Bridge

The distant past played a part in a recent decision taken by Ottawa's city council. A new footbridge was built between Somerset Street East and the University of Ottawa, and a name was being sought for it by the city council, Several sides emerged: those who wanted to honour Ottawa's past and those who wanted to honour more or less recent public figures or institutions.

While the Rideau was being built, the area known as Corktown was home to many of the Irish labourers who actually built the canal; suffered the mosquitos, the heat and cold; and gave their lives so the canal could be completed. There is no doubt that it was a slum as slums went in the early nineteenth century, much worse than what we consider slums today—no sewers, no water, little medical care and a haven for criminal behaviour. Altogether, it was a place for the residents of the Upper Town to avoid. The suggestion "Corktown Bridge" was promoted by the Bytown Museum and the Ottawa District Labour Council. Names suggested by the *Ottawa University Gazette* included the "Bytown Bridge" and the "Tabaret Bridge."

The bridge was well received in September 2006 despite criticisms over its $5 million cost. Suggestions were asked for in January 2007

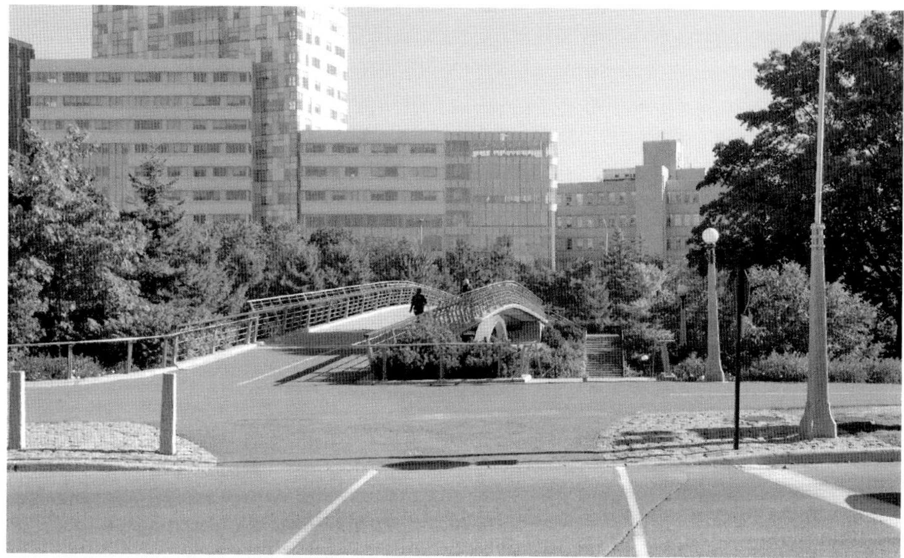

The Corktown Bridge commemorating Irish workers. *Author's collection.*

so that a decision could be taken by March in time for the "official" opening of the bridge in July. Another name suggested took after ex-mayor Charlotte Whitton, and the various suggestions were to be put before the city council. When the council considered the matter, there was an obvious winner. The name "Corktown Bridge" won hands down, and so it came to pass. This is simply one indication that Ottawa respects its heritage and prefers a name that reaches back to the past rather than one honouring individuals and institutions, no matter how deserving they might be.

Local Museums

Ottawa is very fortunate in having many national museums in the city, but the smaller museums that specialize in local history sometimes get overlooked. This chapter will focus on two of these museums, both housed in buildings that are important in our local history in their own right: the Bytown Museum and the Billings Estate Museum.

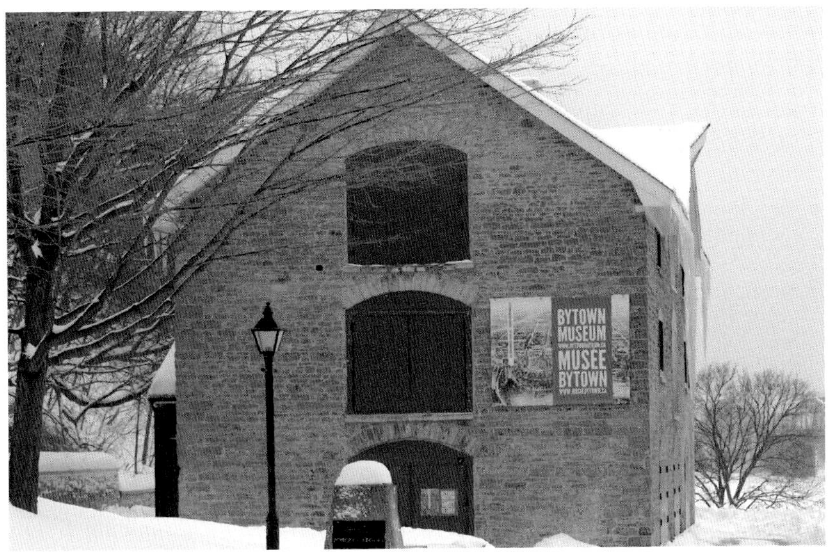

The oldest surviving stone building in Ottawa, circa 1826, now the Bytown Museum.

The Bytown is housed in Colonel John By's storehouse (commissariat), built in 1826. It is the oldest stone building in the city and stands just below Parliament Hill, across from the Chateau Laurier and alongside the canal that has now been declared a World Heritage Site by UNESCO. For the past few years, it has operated independently rather than belonging to the Historical Society of Ottawa, as it was since the 1950s.

The Billings Estate Museum is found just outside the downtown area, but it is one of the oldest residents in the city. Its owners were heavily involved in early events in Ottawa. The Billings estate sits high on the south bank of the Rideau. Originally the home of the Billings family, it is now owned and operated by the city. Do you like taking part in a traditional English tea, with clotted cream and scones? If so, you can sit and enjoy being served tea and goodies every Sunday on the museum lawn. On the grounds of the museum, they serve an authentic tea under a canopy just as citizens did in the nineteenth century. The museum has a fascinating collection of family artifacts that demonstrate the life and times in early Ottawa. It also has educational programs available. (For further details, you can visit the museum website at www.billingsestatemuseum.org.)

In the summer of 2012, the Bytown Museum celebrated its 95th anniversary and the 180th anniversary of the opening of the Rideau

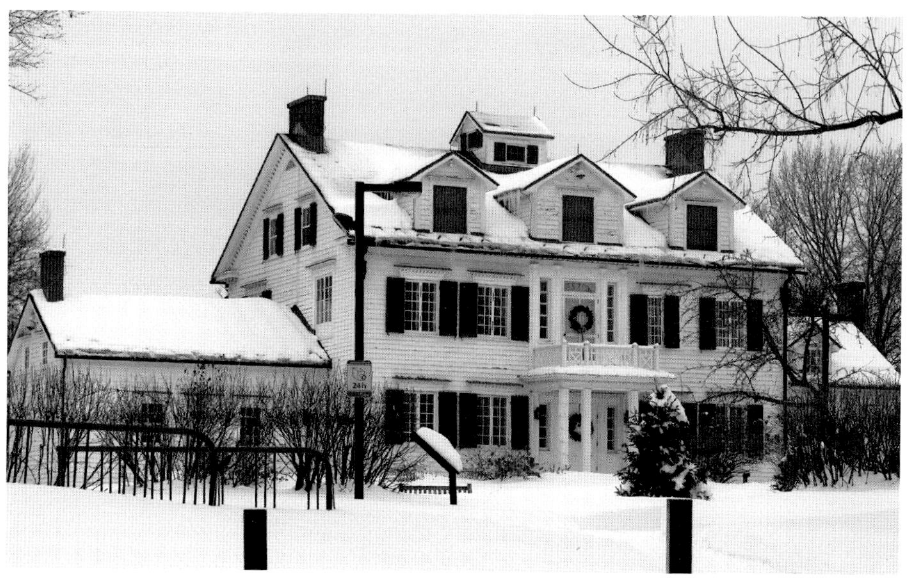

Home of one of the earliest settlers in what is now Ottawa, now the Billings Estate Museum.

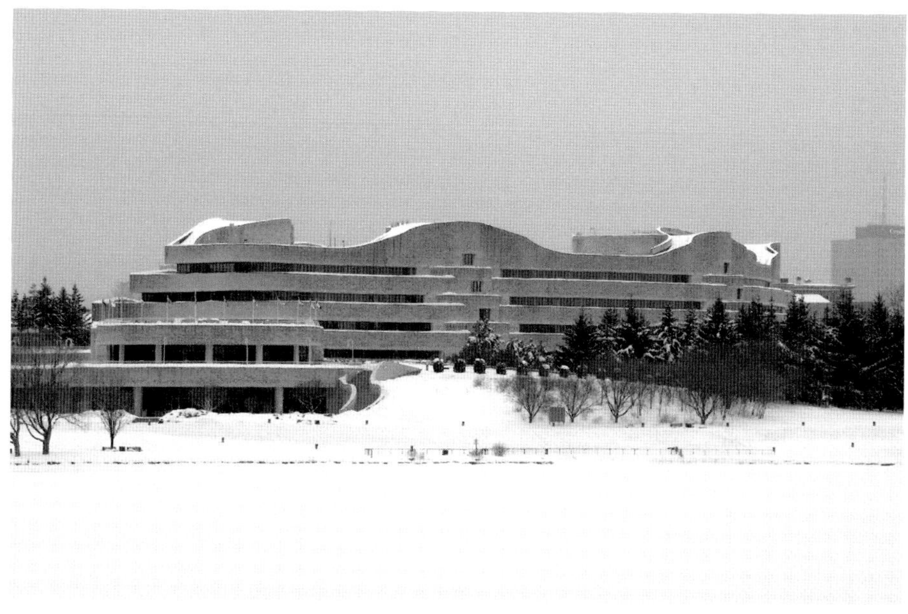

The newly named Museum of History on the Quebec side of the Ottawa River—a Heritage Fairs site in 2013 and 2014.

Canal. The Bytown Museum celebrated the former with an entirely new collection of exhibits. The exhibits also celebrate the 182nd anniversary of the completion of the Rideau Canal. Once you have perused the various exhibits and artifacts, there are other programs that make the visit entertaining at a very low cost. From July until the end of August, if you visit the museum at 1:00 p.m. on summer Saturdays, there are workshops to educate and entertain you. Topics include heritage rug-making and the techniques in photographing heritage buildings. You can also learn more about the music of Corktown—the name given to the Irish workmen's settlement, where the newly named footbridge crosses the canal between Somerset Street and the University of Ottawa.

Another major summer event also takes place at the Bytown Museum on the first Monday in August. This is the day that has been established as Colonel By Day, in honour of Ottawa's founder and the person who gave Ottawa its first name: Bytown. The Bytown Museum and the Council of Heritage Organizations in Ottawa jointly sponsor this event. Colourfully costumed characters are there to greet you, and the admission to the museum is free. There is always music, and dancing is always encouraged.

The Bytown Museum also has guided tours of the premises each day at 1:00 p.m., with museum staff recounting colourful tales of the early days. You can visit the treasure room and perhaps catch a glimpse of the resident ghost, Duncan McNabb. While you take the tour, children can visit the heritage playroom on the third floor, where they can try to master the nineteenth-century toys on display. They can try on historic costumes and have their pictures taken. Would they like to be a lumberjack like Big Joe Mufferaw or a dignified Victorian lady in fine dress? They can "take the King's shilling" and don a red coat like Lieutenant Pooley of the Royal Engineers. There are also educational workshops that teach you to write with a quill pen and seal your letters with the traditional wax seals of the earlier centuries. These activities will take place on weekdays at 11:00 a.m. and 2:00 p.m. (Check out the museum's website at www.bytownmuseum.com.)

These are only a few of the activities taking place in the summer months at locations that stress local history. The area down by the locks is really worth a visit to get some of the flavour of Ottawa in the early days. Many have visited the lock system to see how it works, and there has been a 40 percent increase in tourism forecasted within the next few years. You can also visit the Celtic cross, which commemorates all the labourers who died building the Rideau Canal.

The Natural History Museum, built in 1912.

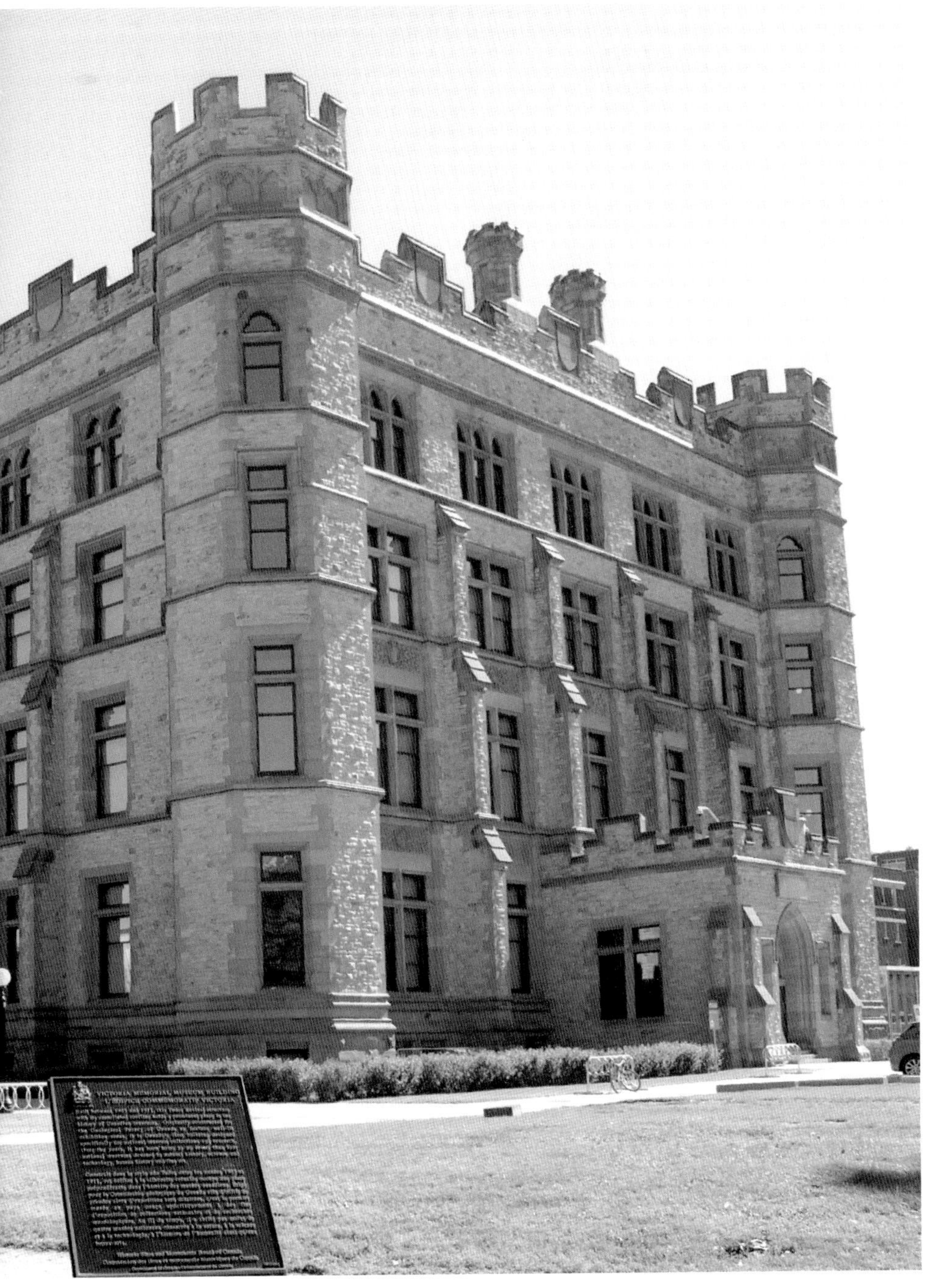

Let's not forget that other museums exist. The big ones are the Museum of Natural History on Gladstone Avenue and the Canadian Museum of History, which sits on the Quebec side of the river but is very visible from the rear of Parliament Hill. Then there is the Museum of Science and Technology on St. Laurent Boulevard. Couple the five museums mentioned with others, and you have a collection of sites at which you could spend days visiting if you like displays, collections of old artifacts and programs developed to meet all historical tastes, even those of children. We live in a historical city, and that fact should be celebrated.

How the Streets Got Named

Considering how many people in Ottawa are new to the city, it seemed reasonable to do a little research and find out who or what some of the oldest Ottawa streets are named after. The book *Ottawa: Making a Capital* has a good section written by Serge Barbe, a member of the city archives, on this very subject. Many persons who contributed to the foundation and growth of our city are not well known, and it is understood that both city staff and the Historical Society of Ottawa have developed tentative plans to make early Bytowners or Ottawa citizens better known. This is a project deserving support. No section of this size can hope to do much more than scratch the surface of this topic. So only a few streets are covered.

Much has been said and written about the proper use of Lebreton Flats, which contained Lebreton Street. These were named after Charles Lebreton (1779–1848), who was a native of Jersey and one of Nepean Township's earliest settlers. He came to our area from Newfoundland and served with distinction in the War of 1812. With a partner, he purchased Lebreton Flats in 1820 and in 1826 got into a legal wrangle with Colonel By and the governor-general, Lord Dalhousie, over the price he wanted for his land. He spent a good deal of money defending the legality of his landownership against the government of the day. He retained his land, but the Rideau Canal was built elsewhere, probably because Dalhousie and By rather disliked him after the court battle. Did sour grapes affect the location of the canal?

Nicholas Sparks (1792–1862), for whom Sparks Street is named, is much better known; however, the extent of his good works in Ottawa is less known.

Sparks came to Canada in 1816 from Ireland to avoid religious strife. He married the widow of Philemon Wright Jr. in 1826. He owned a sawmill and vast timber rights in the area. In 1821, for the equivalent of $500, he purchased land that extended from what is now Wellington Street to Laurier Avenue West and from Waller Street to Bronson Avenue. He sold part of his land to construct the Rideau Canal, but because of the price he asked, another ninety-six acres were expropriated, much to his chagrin. Perhaps wishing to avoid religious strife in Canada, he donated land for churches to both the Anglicans and the Presbyterians. Sparks went on to serve for many years in local government. He named a street on his land after a friend, Daniel O' Connor, who became treasurer of the Dalhousie District (later Ottawa-Carleton), and another after his son-in-law, James Slater.

Slater Street was first named Waugh Street, after a local merchant Caldwell Waugh. James Slater came to Canada in about 1830, married Nicholas Sparks's daughter in 1847 and went on to be, successively, provincial land surveyor, superintendent of the Rideau Canal and chairman of the Ottawa School Board.

Robert Bell (1821–1873) was a promoter of railway construction, a land surveyor and, eventually, a journalist. He bought the *Bytown Packet* in 1849 and changed the name to the *Citizen* two years later. He sold the paper in 1865 to I.B. Taylor. One of the people from whom he originally bought the paper, Henry J. Friel (1823–1869), served as mayor of Bytown in 1854 and mayor of Ottawa in 1857, 1863, 1868 and 1869. Pictures of both Bell and Friel are available at the city archives. Both had streets named after them.

In Lower Town, Bruyere Street is named after Mother Elizabeth Bruyere (1818–1876), the founder of the Grey Nuns and the Ottawa Hospital. She also established an orphanage, a hospice and an asylum for destitute women.

Guigues Street is named after Monsignor Joseph-Eugene-Bruno Guigues (1805–1874), Ottawa's first Roman Catholic bishop. He founded what became the University of Ottawa on land donated by Louis Besserer.

Farther west, Bronson Avenue was named after Erskine Henry Bronson, a prominent businessman whose father, Henry Bronson, had founded a local lumbering firm. Speaking of the lumber business, who else could Booth Street be named after other than J.R. Booth, the "Ottawa Valley Lumber King"? What was originally Naria Street was renamed Laurier after Sir Wilfred Laurier, who was prime minister of Canada from 1896 to 1911.

KEEPING HERITAGE ALIVE: OTTAWA'S HERITAGE FAIRS

For those of you who love history like I do, the annual Heritage Fairs held in Ottawa are an ideal opportunity to come and see what our children think of Canadian history and see the value they place on it. As a historian, I am often disturbed at the state of the teaching of history in our Canadian classrooms. History used to be a compulsory subject many years ago. Now it has become an optional subject where it exists at all.

The Historical Foundation and its annual fairs are an attempt to reverse this attitude by encouraging an interest in history among our youth. Since 2002, both regional and provincial Heritage Fairs have taken place in the Aberdeen Pavillion, Immaculata High School, Cartier Square Drill Hall and the National Museum of Civilization.

On April 4, 2007, the Canadian War Museum hosted the Ottawa Regional Heritage Fair, while the Provincial Fair took place at the National Library and Archives on Wellington Street in May of the same year.

The importance of history is undeniable. It is the written record of human behaviour. Individuals or groups are analysed so that an interpretation can be placed on the reasons things were done. Not all interpretations are the same, but the record of what happened is kept. Unfortunately, professional historians too often write to impress other historians rather than to tell the stories of the past accurately. Consequently, the "what," "how" and "why" of things get lost in excessive debate. Maybe this is one reason why history has lost academic priority. Education seems more and more focused on utilitarianism.

History does have a practical use, though. Where else can we learn about the breakthroughs, mistakes and great deeds of our ancestors? In 1992, one our leading businessmen, Linton (Red) Wilson, decided that his children did not know enough about Canadian history. In partnership with the Bronfman family of Montreal, he founded the Historica Foundation. Since 1993 across Canada and since 2002 here in Ottawa, the foundation's Historica Fairs have strived to spark interest in history.

Opposite: Heritage celebration in 2012 on location. *Fair pamphlet.*

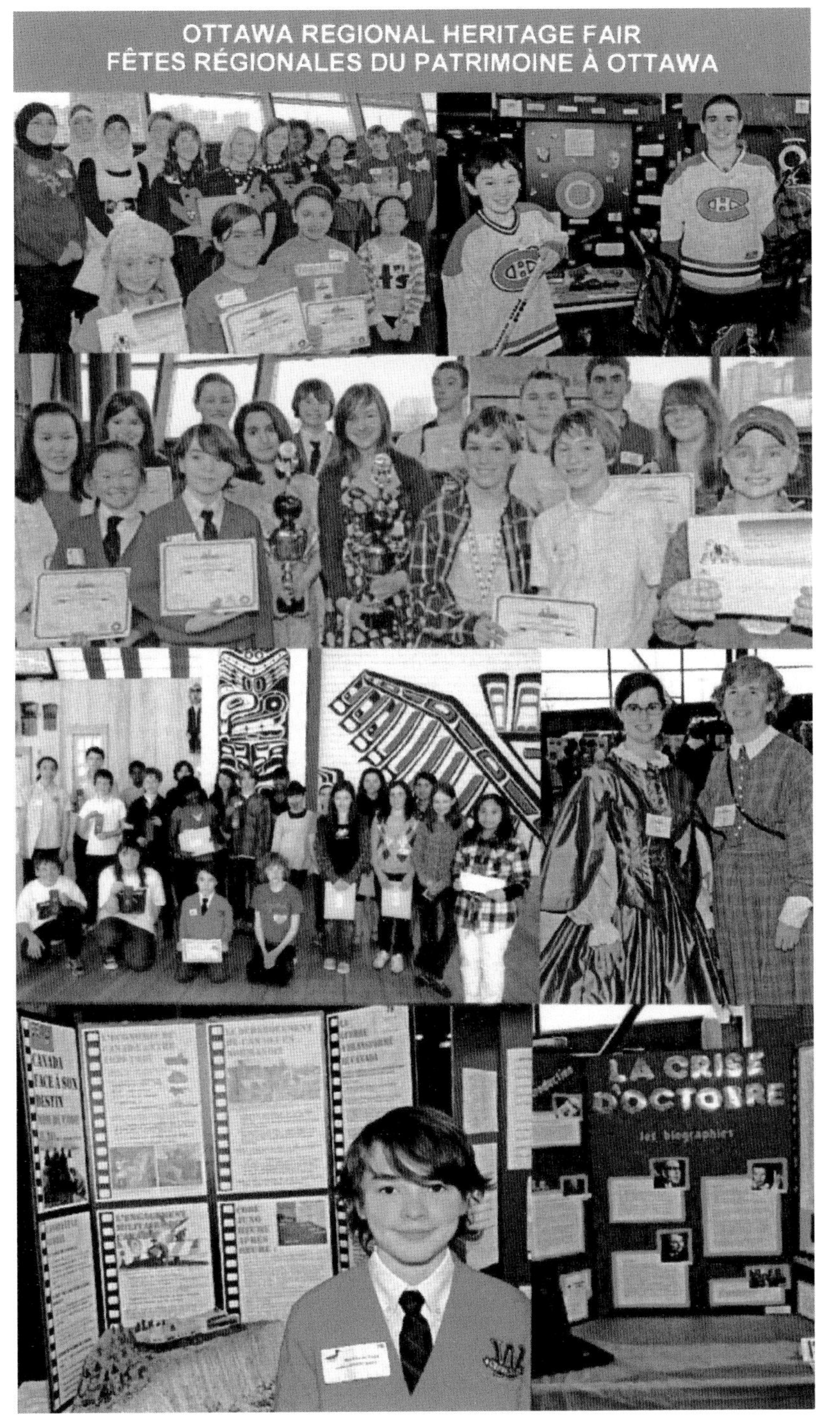
OTTAWA REGIONAL HERITAGE FAIR
FÊTES RÉGIONALES DU PATRIMOINE À OTTAWA
LA CRISE D'OCTOBRE
les biographies

Local schools and school boards are encouraged to sponsor history fairs in individual schools, helped by a regional organizing committee. At least twenty schools in Ottawa are expected to participate in future fairs. Those students will join 300,000 across Canada in developing projects on any topic of Canadian history. Each year since 2002, local organizing committees have sponsored regional fairs where up to 150 projects developed at the school level are exhibited. Prizes and awards are given to all participants. Outstanding projects are selected to proceed to provincial and national fairs in different cities. All travel and living expenses are paid by the Historica Foundation.

At all of these fairs, students are offered workshops on Canadian history and culture and benefit from visiting other parts of their province or country and meeting other students with similar interests. Partners in the process include national and local museums, archives, school boards and private sponsors. In Ottawa, a key grant was made by the Trillium Foundation, while the City of Ottawa, the Historical Society of Ottawa and the Council of Heritage Organizations have also given continuous support. Projects are judged by local educators and heritage experts. Perhaps one day history will become a focus once more in the programs of our educators.

Sources

Artelle, Steven. *The Last Days of Archibald Lampman, Canadian Poet*. Bytown Pamphlet Series, no. 64. Ottawa: Historical Society of Ottawa, 2000.

Careless, J.M.S. *The Rise of Cities in Canada Before 1914*. Canadian Historical Association, pamphlet no. 32. Ottawa: Love Printing Service, Ltd., 1978.

Christie, Dr. A.J. *Rideau Canal and Bytown*. Transcribed in Bytown Pamphlet Series, no. 73. Ottawa: Historical Society of Ottawa, 2012. Original dates to 1827–30.

Desbarats, Linda Scott. *Chapel Court Recollections: The Walter Jachan Series*. Book 2, *The Union Mission and Thomas D'Arcy McGee*. Bytown Pamphlet Series, no. 81. Ottawa: Historical Society of Ottawa, 2012.

Gallaway, Strome, Colonel. *Ottawa's Military History*. Bytown Pamphlet Series, no. 62. Ottawa: Historical Society of Ottawa, 1999.

H. Belden and Company. *The Illustrated Historical Atlas of the County of Carleton*. Toronto: self-published, 1879.

Johnson, Kurt. *Some 1812 Richmond Soldiers/Settlers*. Bytown Pamphlet Series, no. 87. Ottawa: Historical Society of Ottawa, 2013.

Keshen, Jeff, and Nicole St. Onge, eds. *Ottawa: Making a Capital*. Ottawa: University of Ottawa Press, 1999.

Kitchen, Paul. *Dey Brothers' Rinks Were Home to the Senators*. Bytown Pamphlet Series, no. 46. Ottawa: Historical Society of Ottawa, 1993.

Leggett, Robert. *John By: Builder of the Rideau Canal, Founder of Ottawa*. Ottawa: Historical Society of Ottawa, 1982.

———. *Rideau Waterway*. Toronto: University of Toronto Press, 1955.

MacDonald, John A. *A History of the Fenian Raids of 1866 and 1870.* London: London Stamp Exchange, circa 1910–11.

MacKay, Donald. *The Lumberjacks.* Toronto: McGraw Hill Ryerson, 1978.

McCrostie, James. *Being Poor in Ottawa in the Winter of 1891.* Bytown Pamphlet Series, no. 57. Ottawa: Historical Society of Ottawa, 1997.

Nelles, Mike. *Pre-Confederation Healthcare in Bytown.* Bytown Pamphlet Series, no. 70. Ottawa: Historical Society of Ottawa, 2006.

———. *Steamboating on the Rideau Canal.* Bytown Pamphlet Series, no. 71. Ottawa: Historical Society of Ottawa, 2007.

Neville, George A., and Iris. M. Neville. *Rideau Canal and Bytown Memoranda by Dr. A.J. Christie, Physician to the Rideau Canal Works.* Transcribed in the Bytown Pamphlet Series, no. 72. Ottawa: Historical Society of Ottawa, 2007.

Scott, Clifford R. *Robert Bell: A Man for All Seasons.* Ottawa: Historical Society of Ottawa, 2012.

———. *Science in Ottawa: The Early Years.* Bytown Pamphlet Series, no. 67. Ottawa: Historical Society of Ottawa, 2008.

Senior, Hereward. *The Last Invasion of Canada.* Ottawa: Canadian War Museum, 1991.

Serre, Robert. *Early History of Ottawa's Sandy Hill Neighbourhood.* Bytown Pamphlet Series, no. 86. Ottawa: Historical Society of Ottawa, 2013.

Shorter, G.W. *Ottawa-Hull Fire of 1900.* Fire Study no. 7. Ottawa: Division of Building Research, 1962.

Smith, W.H. *Smith's Canadian Gazetteer.* Toronto: H&W Roswell/Coles, 1970.

Snyder, Matt. *Ninety-four Years of the Ottawa Journal.* Bytown Pamphlet Series, no. 60. Ottawa: Historical Society of Ottawa, 1998.

Sulte, Benjamin. *The History of Joseph Montferrand, the Canadian Athlete, A.K.A. Joe Mufferaw.* Translation by Iris M. Neville in the Bytown Pamphlet Series, no. 74. Ottawa: Historical Society of Ottawa, 2008.

Taylor, John H. *Ottawa: An Illustrated History.* Toronto: James Lorimer and Company, 1986.

Walker, Harry, and Olive Walker. *Carleton Saga.* Ottawa: Runge Press, 1971.

About the Author

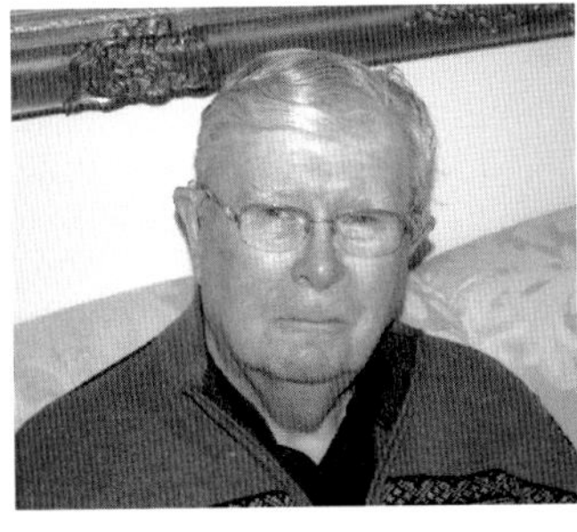

Cliff Scott has been a resident of Ottawa since 1954. He has served in the Royal Canadian Air Force and the public service sector of Canada and has taught history at the University of Ottawa. He attended the University of British Columbia, Carleton University and Ottawa University. He is a student of Canadian and American history, as well as the history of science and technology. During his public service, he was a senior executive specializing in human resource management and organization, design and implementation.

Since 1992, he has been active in the voluntary sector, holding executive positions with the Historical Society of Ottawa, the Friends of the Experimental Farm and the Council of Heritage Organizations of Ottawa. Most recently he inaugurated Heritage Fairs in Ottawa and still serves on the Regional Organizing Committee. He has been married for fifty years to the former Dianne Hewitt of Ottawa and Carleton Place, and they have four children and seven grandchildren. He is convinced that a strong knowledge of history teaches us to cope not only with present situations but also with the world around us.